IOWA

HAUNTED CORRIDOR

JOSH AND KATIE HOPKINS

Other Books by Katie Hopkins:

Seeing Spirits: Opening The Empathic Door

Visions From The Afterlife

IOWA
HAUNTED CORRIDOR

BY
JOSH AND KATIE HOPKINS

JOSH AND KATIE HOPKINS

First Edition:
First printing

JOSH AND KATIE HOPKINS

PUBLISHED BY HAUNTED ROAD MEDIA, LLC
www.hauntedroadmedia.com

United States of America

This book is dedicated to the great and
haunted state of Iowa and its amazing people.

JOSH AND KATIE HOPKINS

ACKNOWLEDGMENTS

We want to thank everyone who contributed to the ghost stories of this book.

Alex Schulte and Jake Truemper from the local radio station KZIA Z102.9 for their story contributions to the Douglas Mansion (The History Center) section. Adam Hyatt, Sarah Hyatt and Vicki Noah for their story contributions to the Granger House Victorian Museum chapter, and Morgan J. East for her story contribution to the Coe College section.

We also want to thank the Granger House Victorian Museum and the Benton County Historical Society for allowing us to use photographs from their archives. Their cooperation and support has been incredible!

The Granger House Victorian Museum is pictured on the cover of this book.

TABLE OF CONTENTS

JOSH AND KATIE HOPKINS

INTRODUCTION

"History is just one big ghost story," this is a quote from Jeff Belanger during a Ted Talk about history and the paranormal.

Without history and more importantly documented history, we as paranormal investigators would go into an investigation blind and would not have documentation to validate our experiences. With a field that is already not scientifically proven, *we need* history to back-up our experiences. History provides a catalyst for hauntings; it is the fuel and we as investigators are the flame.

If you really think about it, one of the most well-known hauntings in Iowa is the Villisca Axe Murder House. The history of the home is that eight people, that included six kids, were murdered on the morning of June 10, 1912. This tragedy took Titanic out of the headlines. That is important history to know going into an investigation at this home, and nonetheless, the trigger that brings thousands of people to the home every year to look for ghosts. The murders are just one little bit of the history of this incident, there is the killer, there is the time that the murders happened, the motive, etc. that all ties into the haunting. What we are getting at here is the main event of the murders is what first catches people's eye to make the trip to the small town of Villisca. The event of the murders is the history. This is what created the ghost stories of the Villisca Axe Murder House. We will say though, we do not believe the Moore family, or the Stillinger girls haunt the home. We believe that what is in that home has been brought in or it is residual energy from the murders. There have been so many different séances, and investigations conducted in that home, that I'm sure there are multiple portals that have opened there.

You could really dive in and look into a larger scale historical event too, such as the Battle of Gettysburg. This very well-known historical event conjures up so many ghost stories, some relevant to the history and some not relevant to the history. This is where documented history comes into play when investigating. What I mean by this is, knowing fact from fiction or myth from reality. For example, many believe that John Wesley Culp, a Confederate Soldier, but originally from Gettysburg, died on his uncle's property called Culp's Hill. Before the Battle of Gettysburg, he moved south to Virginia and joined the Army from there. His unit did fight on Culp's Hill, but this is not where he met his death. He most likely died on Abraham Spangler's property, or one of the farms far to the east of Culp's Hill. Why is this important? If you are going to Culp's Hill to look for John Wesley Culp, you may not find him (or you might, but history would say to look elsewhere). It would make more sense to find the location east of Culp's Hill to try and communicate with the spirit of John Culp since that is where the history of his death lies.

This book is meant to highlight the history of many locations within the Corridor in Central and Eastern Iowa. It will also examine some important locations in the "outskirts" of Cedar Rapids, Iowa. We want to highlight the history because we want to emphasize how important it is to research when investigating for paranormal activity. It can really "make or break" your investigation. There are a lot of investigators that search for "trigger objects" to take with them on investigations; history can be your trigger object! Or, it can lead you to accurate trigger objects!

Again, some of these locations are known to have documented paranormal activity from paranormal investigations. There are also locations in this book that have not had paranormal investigations conducted, and the ghost stories are second and third-hand stories, and more than likely do not have documented history to back-up the claims. These second and third-hand stories would be urban legends or folklore hauntings. We will clarify this at the beginning of each chapter.

Let's explore Iowa's Haunted Corridor!

JOSH AND KATIE HOPKINS

CHAPTER 1

VINTON, IOWA

Vinton, Iowa is the county seat for Benton County. Its history goes back much before the town was founded in 1849. Vinton has become a large river community over the years.

Vinton was known as Northport in the mid-1800s. Many farmers found their settlement in Vinton due to its rich soil and they needed a place to sell their products, as well as purchasing their necessities. Many businessmen came to Vinton in search of prosperity and opportunity. An abundance of factories, farming products and retail stores were built.

John Tilford was a prominent figure in the creation of Vinton and its growing population. He purchased and sold lots for homes and businesses. He donated much of his territories to churches and other community resources. By the early 1900s, the population had increased to around 5,000 people.

Many people reminisce about the thriving times of the 1940s and 1950s. The Iowa Canning Company put on the Sweet Corn Day every Labor Day.

In 2017 the reported population of Vinton was 5,114 people.

The Frank G. Ray House & Carriage House

Photo is of Frank and Emma Ray. Courtesy of Benton County Historical Society.

Frank G. Ray was born on December 31, 1851 in Portland Township, Illinois. Ray grew up on a farm and attended school regularly each winter until he was eleven (Harlan, 1931). He took a four-year break, and then eventually began his education again in the winter months. He ended his education at Oberlin College of Ohio. There is not much history known about his childhood, but there is a very rich history to his adulthood. When he came to Vinton in 1873, he worked in a local implement house. In 1875, he began his own implement store with his business partner. He had a store in Vinton and one in Spencer. He was one of the most successful businessmen in Benton County, Iowa. He was a dealer in farm machinery, he would join an implement and coal business and in 1884 he bought out his partner in the Vinton Store, and he operated it until 1909 when he sold it. His most notable business though was the Iowa Canning Company. It was the largest canning company in the world, and this is where he would make his fortune.

After his retirement in 1909, he didn't stop with his business efforts. He became a director of the Northwestern Portland Cement Company in Mason City, Iowa (Harlan, 1931). Around 1914 he became one of the founders and directors of the Trinity Portland Cement Company, with headquarters in Dallas, Texax (Harlan, 1931). There was also factories in Houston and Fort Worth. He also was the president of the Virginia Gay Memorial Hospital (Harlan, 1931). He was one of the founders of the State Bank of Vinton in 1891, becoming a member of the first Board of Directors (Harlan, 1931). He eventually became president of the bank after the death of Paul Carrell (Harlan, 1931).

Ray married Emma Whiteside from Pomeroy, Ohio on September 13, 1876 at Whiteside's parent's home (Harlan, 1931). They had two children, Earl and Belle.

Photo is of Emma and Belle Ray. Courtesy of Benton County Historical Society.

While in Vinton, he would build one of the most extravagant homes in the community. In 1882, he purchased land to build his home; however, construction didn't begin until 1893. He allowed the basement and foundation to "cure" before he built the home. The home was designed by Murphy and Wallace and was finished in 1894.

The architecture was in that of Queen Anne style. Many characteristics seen within Queen Anne style are "peaks", turrets or towers, eclectic, asymmetry, contrast, surface textures, and bold colors (a Victorian Era characteristic). The materials used were typically patterned brick or stone, even though the homes were usually built with wood which allowed the designer unconstrained artistic expression in patterns and details, wood shingles, slate, and even sometimes stucco. One misconception with Queen Anne style is that many believe it to be from the origins of Queen Anne. This is not true; it is actually based on much earlier English buildings that were generally constructed during the Elizabethan and Jacobean eras. The Elizabethan era was during the reign of Queen Elizabeth I from 1558-1603 and the Jacobean era was during the reign of King James I from 1603-1625. It would take a few centuries for the Queen Anne style to make its way to the United States. The first Americans saw the Queen Anne style of architecture at the Philadelphia Centennial in 1875.

The Ray House has a three-story turret, 10 rooms, seven fireplaces, an open stairway, full floored attic on the third floor, stained glass windows, servant's quarters and full basement, where it is thought they did most of the cooking. The front doors are all made of red oak.

Frank G. Ray died in 1935 at the University of Iowa Hospital in Iowa City, Iowa, from an on-going illness.

The home was placed on the National Register of Historic Places on December 10, 1982. It is now operated by the Benton County Historical Society.

The Haunting of the Frank G. Ray House

There have been multiple paranormal teams to investigate the Ray House. Many of the experiences that people claim to have are seeing shadow people, movement of objects, unexplained light sources, flashlights turning on and off by themselves, hearing footsteps, seeing full bodied apparitions, collecting electronic voice phenomena (EVP), and also collecting video of unexplained flashes of light.

The paranormal teams that have investigated the Ray House also claim to have personal experiences while there. These include, being touched and also feeling a shift in their energy.

The Vinton Train Depot & Rail Museum

The Cedar Rapids & St. Paul Railroad was established in 1865 after the promised route to the Cedar Valley from Cedar Rapids to Vinton did not work out. In 1867, the Cedar Rapids & Burlington Railroad was created, and eventually turned into the Burlington, Cedar Rapids & Minnesota Railroad. The railroad came to Vinton on December 14, 1869 where the commuters were treated with an oyster dinner.

Construction began on the train depot on August 1, 1899 and would be completed and dedicated on March 1, 1900 at the cost of $40,000. The lower walls are made of limestone from a quarry near Postville, Iowa. Inside the depot you can still see the original terrazzo tile floors, white oak wainscoting and the Vinton manufactured pressed tin ceiling panels. A porcelain lamp still hangs over the agent/telegrapher's desk that was there when it was built.

Photos Courtesy of the Benton County Historical Society

Scheduled passenger services would end in 1967. The Benton County Historical Society would be given the depot and it was placed on the National Register of Historic Places in 1990.

This would become one of Eastern Iowa's finest preserved passenger train stations. Today you can see hobo monikers in the motorcar shed.

A hobo moniker is graffiti on a freight car or freight train created by hobos or train workers. Usually the design represented where they came from or it was the date the moniker was produced.

The depot is open for tours and paranormal investigations by appointment. You can contact the Benton County Historical society to setup a tour.

The Haunting of the Vinton Train Depot

You're probably thinking, "It's a train station. What other history can it have other than being a train station?" Well you're right, it is just a train station; however, we need to look past that, look further and think about how many people passed through this train station. The depot has so many different energies embedded into its walls from the many passengers that passed through the depot. It's not just about tragedies.

There are multiple factors that can make up a haunting. A haunting can be residual, so it is like a record player repeating itself overtime. It can repeat itself every second, minute, hour, day, week, year, etc. A lot of the time a residual haunting is residual energy from a certain period. This is more than likely the case at the Vinton Train Depot.

There are also intelligent hauntings in which a spirit can interact with the living. A lot of the time intelligent hauntings stem from a tragic end, but there still can be an intelligent haunting from those who expected to pass. It just means they haven't quite crossed yet.

Some of the claims people have stated are seeing shadow figures, unexplained light sources, hearing unexplained footsteps and other noises, seeing full bodied apparitions, and collecting a magnitude of electronic voice phenomenon (EVP). The difference between a shadow figure and an apparition is that a shadow figure does not typically have features; it is just a shadow of a spirit. An apparition has physical features when you can typically make out certain characteristics of the spirit. This sometimes allows you to compare what you saw with photographs of people tied to that location in history. From the claims, this indicates there is a residual haunting at the Vinton Train Depot.

Some paranormal investigations have been performed at the old train depot in Vinton. The investigation teams that posted their findings claim they heard disembodied voices, caught electronic voice phenomena and even saw shadow figures.

CHAPTER 2

WALFORD, IOWA

"Our Piece of Heaven" read the old town welcome for the small town of Walford. Why do I include this town in this book? It is my hometown where I grew up. It is the town of Walford where I had my first ever paranormal experience at my neighbor's house when I was 10.

Walford was not always called Walford; it started out as the town of Terry. Terry was founded in 1884 when the Chicago, Milwaukee and St. Paul Railroad was extended to that point. The most recent population of 1,450 was recorded in 2018.

This chapter is going to be structured a little differently, since the location that will be discussed no longer exists. However, the land that the general store occupied could still have spirits lurking.

There is actually a lot of history to Walford. Unfortunately, a lot of it is not documented. The most

JOSH AND KATIE HOPKINS

infamous history in the little town of Walford was the murder of Edward Murray in February 1897. The book *Skull in the Ashes: Murder, a Gold Rush Manhunt, and the Birth of Circumstantial Evidence in America* details the Murder of Edward Murray. It follows the new county attorney, M. J. Tobin on his investigation of the fire that occurred at Frank A. Novak's General Store. Many believed it was Frank that perished in the fire. However, after investigation, Tobin comes to find it is not Frank Novak, but the remains of town drunkard Edward Murray. Tobin in fact he is trying to convict Frank Novak for the murder. However, all he had was circumstantial evidence. At this point in time in history, only a few murder convictions had been won on circumstantial evidence in the United States.

Photo Courtesy of University of Iowa Press

Here is a little background on Frank Novak: He was born on April 5, 1865 in Webster County, Iowa. He ran a mercantile store in Walford, Iowa.

He had a terrible addiction to gambling and ran his store into a lot of debt. It is said he took out a $30,000 life insurance policy on himself because of his frustration with his financial difficulties. On February 2, 1897 he asked Edward Murray to come to the store where he crushed his skull, robbed him and then burned the store over him to cover up the crime. He then fled the scene and there is evidence that his wife claimed he was the one in the fire, trying to cash out the insurance money. However, insurance companies were not buying it. Novak was chased for six months, spanning 26,000 miles across the continent and to Alaska by Detective C.C. Perrin of Chicago or Denver. Eventually Perrin caught up with Novak who was claiming at that time to be a J.A. Smith. They were able to compare dental records of Novak with his dentist's records from Iowa, and found out it was in fact, Novak.

Novak tried to say that he kept a bottle of whiskey in the store laced with morphine and that he saw Murray drinking it. It was known that Murray was a drinker, but Perrin wasn't buying it. He also claimed that he tried to rescue Murray but was unable to.

In November 1897, Novak was convicted of second-degree murder and put in the Anamosa State Penitentiary.

Novak was very active while in prison. He joined the prison band and even took up photography. He was considered a "model prisoner" and his friends petitioned that he be set free. He was supposed to serve a life sentence but was eventually set free and died in Chicago on July 12, 1930. He was brought back to Cedar Rapids to be buried in his home state. I have tried searching multiple burial records to see where he is buried and have not been successful.

The Haunting of the General Store (Where it once stood)

Growing up in Walford, I always felt it was a comfortable town where little crime happens. You get your few jokester teenagers or even rebel teenagers, but nothing that would say "lock your doors." Even though we always did lock our doors when we were gone, but everyone in Walford, especially your neighbors look after one another.

However, when I would cross the railroad tracks, I would always feel "different." There is the old Ponderosa, a few abandoned houses, and even an old hotel on "that side of the railroad tracks" (how we always used to refer to that side of town). I just always got an eerie feeling when I would pass certain areas over there.

Could this feeling be the residual energy from the deadly fire at Frank Novak's General Store? Possibly. Could it be that there is just more history to that side of town? Another possibility. I honestly can't explain my feelings. I do not know if it was coming from that traumatic event in history, or if there's just more energy to that side of town.

Do I believe that area is haunted? Absolutely. By who, I do not know.

I really wanted to include this chapter with Walford, because Walford is still very near and dear to my heart. It is a small quiet town, and not much happens. If it does, the entire town knows about it. There have been smaller occurrences throughout the years in Walford, but none have been as big as the infamous murder of Edward Murray.

JOSH AND KATIE HOPKINS

CHAPTER 3

MARION, IOWA

Marion, a small city in Linn County Iowa, named after Francis Marion who was a Revolutionary War Hero. Marion was founded as the county seat of Linn County in 1839 before anyone actually lived. In November 1839, the land was surveyed, and in December 1839, lots were presented at public auction. Marion was quickly recognized as a business center in Linn County and by 1855 the population had grown to 1,500 people. In 1919 the county seat was moved to Cedar Rapids.

As transportation by railway was becoming more and more popular, the city of Marion realized that it was crucial to put a train depot in the heart of the city. Marion was an important point for the Milwaukee and St. Paul Railway and in 1887 Marion became the division point for this railroad.

In 2017, the population of Marion was 39,400.

The Granger House Victorian Museum

The Granger House Victorian Museum can be found in the city of Marion, Iowa. Which is just a few miles outside of Cedar Rapids. The Granger House was built in 1848 and the associated carriage house was built in 1879.

Photo Courtesy of the Granger House Victorian Museum

On November 24, 1845, Hubbard Shedd and his wife Anna bought 40 acres of land from Addison Daniels, who previously had purchased the land from George A. Patterson, called the "triangle." (Hull, 2014). The "triangle consisted of the land from the north side of the Granger House and the south side of the present-day Central Avenue from the Linn County Commissioners (Hull, 2014). Shedd and his wife did not stay in the home for very long, and in 1848 they sold the home to

Christian Myers, and Myers attained more land to the north and west. It is unsure if Myers ever lived in the house.

The main section of the home was built in 1848, and additional rooms were added over time. The carriage home still holds a carriage, horse-drawn sleigh, and milk wagon used by the Granger Family.

Pictured: Dora, Earl, Arthur and Louise.
Photo Courtesy of the Granger House Victorian Museum.

The home changed hands multiple times until Earl and Dora Granger rented the home in 1874 and eventually purchased the home on April 13, 1877 from Charles Myers.

Photo Courtesy of the Granger House Victorian Museum

Earl Granger earned his living by raising cattle, and owning a butcher shop and slaughter house. He was also an active board member of the Farmers & Merchants State Bank. He was born in 1836 and died in 1908. Dora Granger was born in 1850 and died in 1937. The Granger's were considered a middle-class family. They lived a humble life and Dora was known for her hospitality and kindness. However, she was also a tough strong-willed German woman.

Earl and Alfred Granger.
Photo Courtesy of the Granger House Victorian Museum

Earl and Dora had a total of seven children. In which only three lived to adulthood. Their children were Mabel (1874-1879), Wesley (1876-1879), Louise (1877-1891), Arthur (1882-1973), Infant Baby Boy (1886), Margarette (1888-1954), and Alfred (1892-1969). It is believed that Wesley, Mabel and Louise died in the home and that their funeral services would have been held in the parlor.

Photo Courtesy of the Granger House Victorian Museum

Alfred Granger
Photo Courtesy of the Granger House Victorian Museum

Margarette Granger.
Photo Courtesy of the Granger House Victorian Museum

Louise passed away from complications with smallpox and died at the age of 14 years old.

Louise Granger.
Photo Courtesy of the Granger House Victorian Museum

Mabel and Wesley both died of diphtheria. Diphtheria causes a thick covering in the back of the throat which is caused by the bacterium Corynebacterium diphtheriae. The infant baby boy was a still born. The death of Dora's children caused her to go into a deep depression and she eventually was bed-ridden. The Music Room on the main floor of the home was made into the master bedroom for Dora while she grieved the loss of her children. Dora could not care for herself during this time, so her older sister Anna Krouse came to take care of her.

As time passed, and Dora was still mourning the death of her children, Anna and Earl ended up having an affair. This did not end the marriage of Earl and Dora. It is said that Dora and Anna weren't on the greatest of terms, but Anna as a result of the affair ended up getting pregnant. The child that she bore was Margarette. Dora raised Margarette as one of her own, in their home. Eventually, when Earl passed away, Margarette would sue Dora for part of Earl's estate.

The Granger home was passed down to the eldest son Arthur, once Dora passed away, who lived there until his death in 1973. The home stayed within the Granger family for 100 years. With Arthur being the last person to own the home, many of the families' belongings stayed within it. Some of the original artifacts include, Earl and Dora's bed, the secretary in the parlor, the piano in the music room, the ice chest in the kitchen, leg braces that belonged to Mabel who had a medical condition that affected her walking, and all of the woodwork in the home is original. The wood in the home is made of pine, however, they wanted it to look like oak, so Earl hired someone to come in and paint all of the wood with a feather to resemble the look of oak.

In the fall of 1973, the house was purchased by the Marion Historical Museum, Inc. for $30,000 (Hull, 2014). The home was placed on the National Register of Historic Places in 1976. The National Register of Historic Places is the official list of the United States historic buildings, districts, sites, structures, and objects worthy of preservation. It was established as part of the National Historical Preservation Act of 1966 and is overseen by the National Park Service (U.S. General Services Administration).

The Urban Legends of the Granger House

There have been a few urban legends or folklore hauntings created about the Granger House. The first that you may come across when searching "haunted Granger House" is the "Lady in White." When discussing the hauntings going on in the home, we talked with Adam Hyatt (Granger House Board President), Vicki Noah (Granger House Board Vice President) and Sarah Hyatt (Paranormal Director of the Granger House). This was one of the first urban legends they debunked for us. A while back they had a mannequin in the upstairs window and someone who passed by said they saw a "Lady in White" in the window. This started the story of a woman who was haunting the home who wears a white dress. We actually got to see the mannequin that people believed to be the "Lady in White." We asked them if they thought maybe the lady in white was eventually created as a tulpa, and they did not believe she was a real spirit in the home.

I want to use this allegation of a spirit in the window, to discuss making sure you really look closely. This began a huge story of a ghost that did not exist in the home. All I had to do was "Google" *Granger House Lady in White,* and there it was, the story of the "Lady in White." The story states, "Locals report that around midnight, the apparition of a woman is sometimes observed in a window at the Granger House. The woman is all in white. People who have seen her report that they look up and there is a woman in the window, and by the time that they realize that they may have seen an apparition, they look back and she is gone." I can't explain why she was "gone," but I will just assume that she really wasn't, but to make it a ghost story, she had to disappear from the window. Could it be that people have possibly seen a woman standing in the window at some point, sure! We never know when Dora, or any of the children may want to see what is going on outside. However, we will get to the real haunting of the Granger House shortly.

The other incorrect story or urban legend is the rumor that Anna Krouse hung herself in the carriage house. This is 100% not true. Anna was from the Monroe Township (present day Toddville), and she died in her home. It is uncertain where the story began that she committed suicide in the carriage house, but it did circulate around and some have used this as their "trigger" to visit the home and look for ghosts. Another point I want to make, make sure you know the *real* history of the deaths in the locations you are investigating. If you would go into the Granger Home and try and use Anna's death as a trigger, you may not get much as the story of her committing suicide is not true. We were able to gather information talking firsthand with those who know the real history. *DO NOT BELIEVE EVERYTHING YOU READ ON THE INTERNET.* Go to the sources that have the history and know the history. It can really help not only the location to tell the family's story, but as a paranormal investigator, it can help you conduct a thorough investigation with real facts to use as triggers.

The Haunting of the Granger House Victorian Museum

Now that we have discussed the urban legends, let's dive into the real haunting of the Granger House, because it is, in fact, haunted. We were able to talk to Adam, Vicki and Sarah about their experiences in the home. Adam has had an encounter in the carriage house, where he saw a full-body apparition. He says he believes it was Earl Granger since he could make out that he was wearing a white coat, which looked like a butcher's coat or apron. This would make sense being that Earl Granger was a butcher and owned a slaughter house. He said he could compare it to a photo of Earl Granger as well. Another spirit that originated in the carriage house is the spirit by the name of Mike. They believe that Mike possibly came from Fort Madison, Iowa, on the train. They do not know exactly what Mike was doing in Fort Madison; he could have just come off of the train since there was a train depot in Fort Madison and in Marion. It is not known if he came from Iowa State Penitentiary. They say he is not harmful and has a good energy. They also said recently he has started to make his way into the house.

The main spirits of the home are believed to be that of the Granger Family. This includes Earl, Dora and the kids. Anna can even be found in the carriage house sometimes. They are not sure why she hangs out in the carriage house; it could be that she doesn't feel welcome in the home due to the infidelity between her and Earl. It could also be that Dora has said, "Proper women do not go in the carriage house," so she may be pushing her there, again, due to the infidelity.

The most common experiences people have had in the Granger House are scratching, footsteps, disembodied voices, and shadow figures. I asked Sarah what the craziest experience was that she had witnessed in the home. She gave me two experiences. The first included her jacket being tugged on while leading a paranormal discussion. Sarah teaches a course called *Seeking the Paranormal* which includes different topics each session. During this session she was up talking to the group and all of a sudden felt her jacket being tugged on. She looked back and waved her hand behind her in a "stop" kind of motion. Not only did she feel the tug, her husband Adam saw her jacket moving and being pulled down in a tugging motion. They believe this to be one of the children trying to get Sarah's attention. Another experience with children in the home is hearing a little girl singing upstairs. They believe this to be either Louise or Mabel.

Mabel has also been known to move things throughout the house. As mentioned before, she had leg braces, they are still in the home, and can be seen in her room today.

The leg braces used to be down on the main floor in the sitting area. One day, they were going through the home and could not find her leg braces. They looked everywhere and could not find them. They went upstairs and were looking around and still could not find them.

They went into Mabel's room, and were looking around, and of all places, they found the leg braces behind the door of Mabel's room. Could this have been Mabel being silly, or saying she wanted her leg braces close by? Today the leg braces are kept on her bed, along with a few other Granger Family belongings.

Vicki has also encountered the family and Mike. She said that she witnesses the common experiences often while in the home.

A very important thing to mention about this haunting is that it is a very comfortable haunting. It is just the Granger Family living their everyday life in the present day. Some of the haunting is residual and some is intelligent. While the Granger House is very haunted, it is never menacing or uncomfortable. Sarah stated, "It is great for a first investigation for someone just starting out in the paranormal field."

The Granger House Victorian Museum is open to the public on Saturday and Sunday from 1:00 PM - 4:00 PM. They host multiple events open to the public, some paranormal and some non-paranormal. It is also open for private paranormal investigations by appointment.

JOSH AND KATIE HOPKINS

CHAPTER 4

IOWA CITY, IOWA

Iowa City, Iowa was created on January 21, 1839 by an act of Legislature from the Legislative Assembly of the Iowa Territory (Think Iowa City, 2019). The capitol had been in Burlington, Iowa and at the yearning of Governor Robert Lucas, it was moved to Iowa City.

On May 1, 1839, Chauncey Swan and John Ronalds (Commissioners) met in Napolon (just south of present-day Iowa City), to choose a site for the new capitol city (Think Iowa City, 2019). Iowa City was chosen as the territorial capitol in 1839, but would not become the capitol city until 1841, after the construction of the capitol building began. Eventually, the capitol of Iowa would be moved to Des Moines in 1857.

Iowa City is the home of the second largest state university, The University of Iowa (Iowa Hawkeyes). A few buildings will be discussed that reside on the campus of the University of Iowa in this chapter.

In 2017 the population of Iowa City was 75,798.

The University of Iowa

The University of Iowa was founded in1847. It is the home of the Iowa Hawkeyes. It is the second largest university in the state of Iowa. It currently is organized into 11 colleges and offers more than 200 areas to study and has seven professional degrees (PhD).

The University of Iowa is most known for its programs in health care, law and the fine arts.

On February 25, 1847, the University of Iowa was founded, just 59 days after Iowa was admitted into the Union. The legal name of the university was the *State University of Iowa*, but the Board of Regents approved *The University of Iowa* in 1964. The first instruction by faculty was offered in March of 1855. There were 124 students, 41 of these students were women. In 1856-57 the university grew to nine departments which offered ancient languages, modern languages, intellectual philosophy, moral philosophy, history, natural history, mathematics, natural philosophy and chemistry. The first president of the university was Amos Dean.

The original campus was 10 acres and on top of that was the Old Capitol Building. The cornerstone was placed on July 4, 1840 and housed the Fifth Legislative Assembly of the Territory of Iowa, this made Iowa City the capitol of the state of Iowa on December 28, 1846. It had previously been the third capitol of the territory of Iowa. In 1857, the capitol was moved to Des Moines, and it was made the permanent home of the University.

Slater Hall (University of Iowa)- The Urban Legend of the Axe Man

Josh and I being huge Hawkeye fans, we have to at least talk about one allegedly haunted building from the University of Iowa campus that has had ghost stories being told about it for many years. However, the building alone is just under 60 years old. Slater Hall was built in the 1960s as a 12-story housing facility. It is the only residence hall named after an Iowa athlete.

University of Iowa | digital.lib.uiowa.edu/ictcs
Photo Courtesy of the University of Iowa Libraries

Slater Hall is named after Fred "Duke" Slater, who was an Iowa Football player from 1918-1922. He was named to the all-Iowa team as a freshman and he played 10 years of professional football after graduating from Iowa in 1928 with his law degree. He played for the Milwaukee Badgers, Rock Island Independents and the Chicago Cardinals (yes, those are the teams he played for, I did not get the names wrong). He was the first African American lineman in NFL history, and one of five to be inducted into the Iowa Sports Hall of Fame. In his later years he ended up becoming a Federal Judge in Chicago.

I want to make it clear that the ghost story in this chapter has nothing to do with Fred "Duke" Slater, but I find it important to honor him in this chapter.

On a larger scale of history, the University of Iowa begins back in 1847 when the University was founded. It is the oldest and the second largest university in the state of Iowa. The campus is located on the banks of the Iowa River, with a 1,880 acre campus. It is classified as a Doctoral University, and best known for health care, law and the fine arts. It was the first public university to open as a coeducational school, first coeducational medical school, and was the first to open a Department of Religious Studies at a public university. The Iowa Hawekye athletics are a Division I school in the NCAA and are part of the Big Ten Conference. All in all, the school is widely popular throughout the Hawkeye State! Why am I telling you all of this you ask? Because it's HISTORY! It could potentially be important to research and linking to paranormal activity on the campus.

The Urban Legend of the Axe Man

When I first was reading the claims of the Axe Man and his sightings, I thought to myself, "Why would an Axe Man be in Slater Hall?"

I ran the claims through my head and even the "alleged tragedy" of what happened. The folklore is that a man jumped from the 9th floor, ultimately ending his life. There is no documentation of this incident, and I am not sure where the story originated, but it has been around for quite some time!

I sat and I pondered the idea of how an Axe Man could be haunting the hall. I kept thinking, "Well, could the thought and belief of the Axe Man being there for so many years, create a haunting?"

I reached out to my fellow colleagues and Haunted Road Media authors, Mike Ricksecker, Vanessa Hogle and Adam Tillery. These are their thoughts.

I messaged Mike on Facebook and said, "I am writing about urban legends as well in the Corridor book. Even though they are urban legends or folklore hauntings, do you feel they can trigger activity because of the 'thought' of the stories? Almost like the chatter of the certain story can bring spirits out? For example, there is a dorm at the University of Iowa, Slater Hall, and the urban legend is that a guy jumped from the 9th floor and killed himself and now he haunts the 9th floor, and throughout the years has been given the name Axe Man because, apparently, he carries around an Axe. Students claim to see him, etc. but this is just an urban legend. Do you feel the talk of it could have sparked a haunting? Basically, the talk of a haunting created a haunting."

Yes, that is the lengthy message I sent to Mike, and his response was, "It could be that energy manifesting itself into things people want to see or what many people call a tulpa. A tulpa is a type of entity that discovers stories like this and takes on the persona of the legend even though the original legend isn't true. Ironically, I'm doing a Friday Night Ghost Frights (FNGF) on Slender Man this week which some believe is now a tulpa even though it never existed to begin with."

Adam also brought up a tulpa, and the idea of Slender Man and creation of him from the belief in him. He stated it could be the tulpa effect. The tulpa effect is defined as being a thought form or being created from collective thoughts of separate individuals. It derives from a Tibetan word "tulpa" which means to construct or to build or create a manifestation. An imaginary friend could also be a tulpa.

Vanessa too was also on board with the belief that spirits can manifest from a tulpa.

Is a tulpa what is responsible for the claims of Slater Hall being haunted? It could be. Could it also be a real haunting? It could be. However, in this case, it has been deemed an urban legend that I'm sure will haunt Slater Hall for many years to come.

The Old Capitol Building (Old Capitol Museum)

Before the capitol of Iowa was moved to Des Moines, it was right in the heart of Iowa, in Iowa City. Now located on the University of Iowa campus next to Macbride Hall, the beautiful and historic capitol building houses multiple exhibits, a Natural History Museum and even can be rented for weddings and special events.

The decision was made on May 4, 1839 to have the capitol be in Iowa City. I want to make it a point to note that Iowa was not a state yet in 1839. So, it was just a territory at this time. Iowa became a state seven years later in 1846. The contract for the design and construction of the new capitol was awarded to John Francis Rague in November 1839. Rague is also the architect that designed the first capitol building in Springfield, Illinois where Abraham Lincoln would have visited while in office as a congressman.

On July 4, 1840, construction began, with the laying of the cornerstone. On July 13, Rague resigned from the project and left Chauncey Swan in charge. Chauncey was one of the commissioners for the territorial government that had chosen Iowa City as the capitol.

The building was built with Devonian limestone, and a majority of that limestone was quarried from the bluffs along the Iowa River, near North Liberty. They were brought down the river on barges and then were transported by oxen to the construction site. The original floor joists, roof trusses and other supporting beams were carved from native oak. Four rooms of the Old Capitol were completed by 1842 and the Iowa Legislative Assembly began to use the building for the first time in December 1842.

The first governor of Iowa, Ansel Brigg was inaugurated in Old Capitol in 1846.

The first governor of Iowa, Ansel Brigg

The University of Iowa was founded in the Old Capitol building on February 25, 1847 (Go Hawkeyes!). The state historical society was also founded in the Old Capitol building on January 25, 1857. Almost a year after the historical society was founded; the capitol of Iowa was moved to the city of Des Moines.

In December 1857, the capitol of Iowa moved to Des Moines, just as the state government had appropriated $4,000 to finish the construction of the Old Capitol building. The move of the capitol to Des Moines made the Old Capitol the first permanent building of the University of Iowa.

From 1857-1863 the Old Capitol building housed the entire University. In 1863 South Hall was used as the second building of the University. A library was opened in 1857 and a museum of natural history in 1858 by Chancellor Amos Dean. They are both located on the second floor of Old Capitol. The building also housed all offices and classrooms. It also included a chapel, an armory, and a fire station.

From 1868-1910 the Iowa Law school of Des Moines occupied the Old Capitol building when the University took over the law school. In 1910, Gilmore Hall was built and the law school moved there.

The Old Capitol underwent significant structural renovations from 1921 to 1924. Steel beams replaced the once oak supporting beams, the spiral staircase had one riser added to it, and the foundation on the southwest side of the building was repaired.

A brass chandelier, weighing 650 pounds was installed in the Senate Chamber and over 6,400 three-inch square pieces of gold leaf were applied to cover the

Old Capitol's dome. Finally, the Old Capitol building was complete.

On July 18, 1970, 130 years after the cornerstone was laid University of Iowa President Willard Boyd declared that the Old Capitol would be restored as a historic monument. From 1970-1976 the restoration project of the Old Capitol was completed. On July 3, 1976, the Old Capitol was reopened as a historic National landmark.

A tragic fire sparked on November 20, 2001 at the Old Capitol. Contractors accidentally started a fire at 8:30 AM in the cupola of the Old Capitol building. It started by using a heat gun during renovations to the cupola. It destroyed the cupola, dome, and bell that was built during the restorations in the 1920s. Thankfully, the items were not damaged beyond repair and were able to be restored. It would take another four and a half years of restorations and renovations before opening back up to the public. It reopened in May 2006 to the public.

Thankfully, there is a lot of history documented of the Old Capitol building. I remember going on trips down to Iowa City with my Grandparents to see the Natural History Museum. We would go down for Kid's Day for to watch the Iowa Football team practice and then go to the Old Capitol. Josh even has ties to the Old Capitol building as one of his relatives used to own it. This relative has been gone for a long time so we never knew them, but it is cool to have that connection to the building!

The Urban Legend of the Old Capitol Building

The claims are that a mysterious man in 1851 came into Iowa City from the train and went to the Old Capitol building. The next morning, he was found dead. It is said that he comes back and haunts the Old Capitol building every October.

This is an urban legend. There are no known deaths at the Old Capitol, especially a murder. Could we go back to this being a tulpa? Sure. However, I don't want to focus on the urban legend to discuss whether or not the Old Capitol is haunted.

This potential haunting ties into energy once again. Think about all of the energy that is embedded into the walls of the Old Capitol from nearly 180 years of people coming and going. Also, think about what the building is made of: limestone! Limestone is a huge energy builder for spirits, so spirits could just be attracted to the old building. Limestone is said to have the ability to absorb and release electromagnetic energies. This could potentially explain why some sites are more haunted than others, or why some spirits have more strength at one location versus another. This also includes water sources. Locations near a running water source could potentially provide more energy for the spirits to manifest and communicate.

So, to conclude the section about the Old Capitol, do I believe that it is haunted by the urban legend? No. Do I believe it's haunted, possibly. What kind of haunting? This is more than likely a residual haunting. In my opinion a majority of hauntings are residual.

Oakland Cemetery

I can't write a book about the Corridor and not include the Black Angel. This is probably one of the most well-known urban legends in Iowa City, if not the entire Corridor, actually the entire state of Iowa!

Josh and I visited the Black Angel in 2016. I am only a short 30-minute drive from Iowa City and this was the first time I had ever visited the Black Angel. I had heard the legends and stories that it used to be looking up to the skies and smiling and used to be a golden bronze in color and eventually turned to black. The Black Angel is an eight-and-a-half-foot tall burial monument for the Feldevert family. It was erected in the cemetery in 1912.

Some things we do know about the Black Angel include: It was established by Teresa Dolezal Feldevert. She was a physician who had immigrated to America from Strmilov, Bohemia. Teresa came to Iowa City with her son, Eddie Dolezal, where she worked as a midwife. They lived in Iowa City until 1891. Eddie died of meningitis at the age of 18 in 1891 and he was buried in

Oakland Cemetery. Teresa had a tree stump monument erected over his grave. It can still be seen today. So, we all know this is viable and true as this is all documented history. The urban legend comes to play when discussing why the Black Angel possibly went under transformation.

Teresa did not stay in Iowa City after Eddie's death. She moved to Eugene, Oregon, and married Nicholas Feldevert, and he died tragically a few years later in 1911. After the death of Nicholas, she moved back to Iowa City and hired Mario Korbel to design the angel monument to hover over her son and the ashes of her husband.

There are many stories as well about when the statue was actually put in the cemetery. Some say it was installed right when it got there in 1912. Others say it was held in a barn for six years and was not put in the cemetery until after Teresa brought a court case against the artist for not making it to her specifications. Whatever the correct story may be, we know that at some point after the installation of the angel, Eddie's monument was moved from its original location to where it is now next to the angel. Eddie's remains, and the ashes of Nicholas Feldevert were placed in a repository under the angel's base.

Teresa ended up dying from cancer on November 18, 1924, and her ashes were also put underneath the angel and this is when the urban legends began.

The Urban Legend of the Black Angel

As it was mentioned previously, legend has it that the statue was a gold bronze when installed and then mysteriously turned to black after a few years of it being installed. The logical theory is that the natural elements took their toll and natural oxidations of the metal made it turn black. The urban legend though is that it turned black from the forces of evil, infidelity and possibly murder.

One of the many legends says that Teresa was mysterious and somewhat evil and that caused the angel to turn black. The odd shadowing was to be a reminder of the sins of her family and is a warning for people to stay away from her grave. Some said that the design of the angel showcases Teresa's ways because it is looking down and the wings are positioned down, when most were looking up to the sky with the wings in an uplifting position. However, this opens up another legend, that the angel used to look up to the heavens, but after Teresa vowed to be faithful to her husband, even after his death, and then wasn't, the position of the angel changed.

Another legend says that if a girl is kissed at the angel's feet in the moonlight that she would die within six months. Other legends say that if you touch the angel on Halloween night it would lead to death in seven years and, even worse than that, kissing the angel itself would cause death.

These are all legends, but I wouldn't even think of testing the limits!

Some say that the angel was struck by lightning the night of Teresa's funeral which caused it to turn black.

The most common legend on why the angel turned black is the story of alleged infidelity. It is said that Teresa vowed to her husband that even after his death she would not love another man and remain faithful to him until the day she died. She told him that the death angel would turn black if she broke this promise.

One of the harshest or unforgiving legends of the angel's color is that Teresa's son did not actually die from an illness. Some say that she murdered him, then fled to Oregon, and later stated that her guilt brought her back to Iowa City. Her guilt weighing on her, she moved her son under the angel, and that when it changed colors to represent her shame. There is no evidence to back up this claim.

While all of these claims have very little evidence of truth, they are a huge part of the folklore and legend of the Black Angel in Oakland Cemetery in Iowa City. The Black Angel is one of the most notable haunted statues, which is likely based on the stories, curses and enigmas attached to the past and present.

Our Visit to the Black Angel – The Haunting

Josh and I went to the Black Angel in October 2016. The vibe you get from looking at it is pretty eerie. I stood under one of the wings, and immediately felt like I needed to move. I was overcome with energy that I can't explain. It wasn't dark, it wasn't light, it was just, energy. Do I believe this is from the legends that were just described? No. I believe what I felt was the energy of the legends. What I mean by this is that the legends are so popular that the energy from people who visit and just the "belief" in the legends stick to the monument. Also, it is known that spirits can visit their graves often, which could also be the reason for an overwhelming energy. So much energy in one place can do that to you.

There are also some mausoleums just down from the Black Angel that have a lot of energy to them and in my opinion have their residents visiting often.

There is also a legend of another Black Angel in Council Bluffs, Iowa.

The Black Angel is one of the most popular legends in Iowa. Many people visit the Black Angel to test the legends and see what "feels" they get from the angel. I do hope that Teresa, Eddie and Nicholas are resting in peace, even with their many visitors they get.

CHAPTER 5

ANAMOSA, IOWA

Anamosa is the county seat of Jones County. It is a very small town of approximately 6,000 people. Jones County is also the home of Edinburgh Manor, which I have written about in my book *Seeing Spirits: Opening the Empathic Door*. Jones County dates back as early as 1840 with the county seat originally being set to be in the small town of Edinburgh. However, the plan fell through and the land where the first court house was going to be built was deeded to the county to build the first county poor farm, from President Buchanan. This is the site of Edinburgh Manor. The first poor farm was just to the right of the current building (Edinburgh Manor). I could go on and on about the Manor as I have had multiple experiences in that building, however, I want to find the hidden haunts of Anamosa. The hauntings that are not talked about on a daily basis.

This brings me to Holy Cross Cemetery.

Holy Cross Cemetery

There are many haunts in Anamosa, Iowa, that are well-known. I don't want to focus on those though, as they have been featured in many books, articles, etc. I am actually going to focus on a cemetery that sits on a hill. It looks peaceful and inviting, until you are informed of the alleged history/urban legends of the cemetery.

Holy Cross Cemetery is located just northwest of Anamosa. There is not much history to be found about Holy Cross Cemetery. However, I wanted to include it in this book because of the feelings Josh and I have had while visiting the cemetery, and also do discuss the urban legend of the cemetery.

The Urban Legend of Holy Cross Cemetery: The Hanging Tree

Legend says that there was a tree that was used to hang Native American's in the Holy Cross Cemetery. The tree is said to still be in the cemetery, which is behind the first group of trees in the back of the cemetery. Some say you can still see the burn marks from the ropes being wrapped around the tree. It is also said to be an old Native American burial ground. If this is true, that alone is all you need for a haunting. Native American burial ground in my opinion can create some of strongest hauntings.

Many have reported seeing shadow figures and even one claims they have seen a reaper like figure in the cemetery.

The claims of paranormal activity include seeing shadow figures, orbs, and also to hear the creaking of a tree branch like someone is being hanged from it.

Our Experiences

The most recent visit to the cemetery was for an interview for a documentary. Josh, my sister in-law, Hannah, my mother-in-law, Joy, and I went to the cemetery to meet the two gentlemen who were creating the documentary. They wanted to interview us about Edinburgh Manor. There are many reasons we didn't go to the Manor, but I will not get into those, so we decided to tell them to meet us at Holy Cross Cemetery.

As we drove into the cemetery, we immediately felt a heavy energy. Now, I want to point out, this does not validate that there was a hanging tree in this cemetery, this is a pretty common feeling in haunted locations. Especially in a cemetery, there are so many different energies that can really "throw off" your own energy.

This is a pretty typical feeling in this cemetery and it only gets worse the farther back you go. This is said to be the area where the hanging tree was. There is no evidence or documentation of the hanging tree. It again is just an urban legend. When you go into the cemetery and you think of the hanging tree it really can affect how you feel. You almost believe in it so much that you are the source of making you be a sponge for the energy in the cemetery. This really goes with any haunting. This also shows that a tulpa does not have to be a "being," it can be something as simple as a tree.

CHAPTER 6

SPRINGVILLE, IOWA

Formerly Brown Township, Springville was founded in 1837 when the Sac and Fox Indian tribes surrendered to the United States Government a stretched-out piece of land in the shape of an arrowhead. This was known as the Second Black Hawk Purchase. In 1838, Charles Pickney staked out a claim of land that included the area where Springville is today. It was given the name the Brown Township in 1839 after Nathan Brown, one of two Revolutionary War Veterans to be buried in Linn County. Brown settled in a village southwest of the present-day Springville.

Nathan Brown was born on July 22, 1761 in White Plains, New York. He started to prepare for the American Army at the age of 14 by practicing drill. He was only 16 when he entered the Army to fight in the Revolutionary War. He first fought in Harlem Flats and his second battle was the Battle of Brooklyn, which was on the current site of the Greenwood Cemetery in New

York. He was wounded in battle, but not seriously hurt. He had seven brothers in the same army and his captain was his uncle. One the war was over he moved to South Hallow and eventually Buffalo, New York. He would finally settle one mile southwest of Springville, Iowa in May 1839. He died on November 25, 1842.

In 1881, a petition was signed by 41 people (365 people were in Springville at this time), to incorporate the city of Springville. It was put to vote on July 20, 1881, and the city limits were approved.

The population of Springville in 2017 was 1,143.

The Springville Cemetery

There is not much history to be found about the Springville Cemetery. The most you can find is there are more than 2,000 people who have been laid to rest there.

However, the town of Springville alone is very historical with a lot of events that create a recipe for a haunting.

The Urban Legend of the Springville Cemetery

You would think out of all the history that there is in the Springville Cemetery, that the haunting and folklore would be based around Nathan Brown. Well, it's not. It is focused around a story about a grave digger that fell to his death while digging a grave. It is said that he fell into the grave and broke his neck. It is said that people have seen him holding a green glowing shovel walking through the cemetery.

JOSH AND KATIE HOPKINS

CHAPTER 7

CENTRAL CITY, IOWA

Central City is located in Linn County. It is just less than 25 miles northeast of Cedar Rapids. It is part of the Cedar Rapids Metropolitan Statistical Area.

It was founded in the 1850s, and its name refers to its location, which is within the proximity of the railroads.

Central City is the home of the Central City Commercial Historic District. This is a small area in the city's downtown. Much of the district was destroyed in a fire in 1889. Many of the local entrepreneurs tried to rebuild the district rapidly. Paul Sigmund was a local contractor and builder that built a group of buildings after the fire. This area was listed on the National Register of Historic Places in 2003.

The population of Central City in 2017 was 736.

The Matsell Bridge is a historic bridge in Central City. It was designed in and construction began in 1870. It was built in stages that took place between 1870 to 1906. The bridge stretches for 303 feet and carries

Matsell Park Road over the Wapsipinicon River. The Bridge was placed on the National Register of Historic Places in 1998.

The bridge is also part of the Matsell Bridge Natural Area. This area is the largest natural area in Linn County, with 1887 acres.

The bridge is named after George W. Matsell. He was a New York City Chief of Police from 1845-1857. There are some stories that say Matsell befriended some American Indians while visiting New York City. His kindness was greatly appreciated by the American Indians and they invited him to visit Iowa. He accepted their invitation and was enamored by the land, which led him to build his own mansion here in Iowa. His home was inspired by President George Washington's Mount Vernon home. His home eventually had 11 buildings which included livestock barns, grain storage, a gatekeepers house and an icehouse. Eventually, the buildings would fall into disrepair and they were demolished. The icehouse and the entrance gate are the only remnants of the Matsell Residence that remain today.

The Urban Legend of Matsell Bridge

When you review the history of the Matsell Bridge the claims of paranormal activity here really do not add up. There is nothing that indicates the haunting could possibly be George Matsell or the American Indians he befriended.

The claims of activity are merely ghost stories that have been created overtime. The legends say that if you drive into the middle of the bridge, your car will shut off on its own and an unforeseen force pushes you across the bridge. It is said that you can hear eerie noises outside of your car, and when you leave, you'll see handprints on the surface of the trunk or back of the vehicle. There are actually a few bridges in Iowa that have these types of claims.

Apparently, if the spirits realize you have been there more than once, they will try and push you off the bridge or even try to break out your car windows.

This is the type of stuff you see in a movie. Anyone who is in the paranormal field and has knowledge of spirits and their energy, knows that it would take way more energy than a spirit actually has to pull something like this off. Or it would take a very powerful type of haunting, which is very rare.

There is nothing within the history that would back these types of claims up either. If you go off of the history of the location, you would not expect such a malevolent type of haunting here, but more of a light, friendly haunting, as therefore, Matsell came to Iowa, from the kindness of the American Indians and his love for the land.

CHAPTER 8

CEDAR RAPIDS, IOWA

In the heart of the corridor lies the city of Cedar Rapids. Cedar Rapids is the second largest city in Iowa, behind Des Moines (the capitol), with a population of approximately 133,000 people.

Cedar Rapids is the county seat of Linn County. The city lies on the banks of the Cedar River and just about 20 miles north of Iowa City. The present-day location of Cedar Rapids was the territory of the Fox and Sac tribes, and the first settler, Osgood Shepherd, arrived in 1838, establishing the territory. The town was first named Columbus by William Stone, and in 1841 it was resurveyed and renamed by N.B. Brown and his associates. They named the town Cedar Rapids after the rapids of the Cedar River. The river was named after the large amount of red cedar trees that grew along the banks of the river. The city of Cedar Rapids was incorporated on January 15, 1849, and in 1870 Cedar Rapids invaded the community of Kingston. There are still remnants of the community of Kingston with the Kingston Neighborhood and with the Cedar Rapids Community School District, naming their football stadium, Kingston Stadium.

The economy of Cedar Rapids flourished in 1871 with the founding of the Sinclair Meat Packing Plant by Thomas Sinclair. His name would become even more well-known when his wife would take her earnings from her husband's death and build an extravagant mansion called "Fairmore" later on to be known as, "Brucemore."

Cedar Rapids also flourished with Douglas Starch Works and Quaker Oats.

Needless to say, there is a lot of history in Cedar Rapids, some good, some bad. The most recent historical events to happen in Cedar Rapids are the Flood of 2008 and Flood of 2016. The flood of 2008 was catastrophic. Many homes were destroyed, and it even hit many historical buildings in the downtown Cedar Rapids area, such as Theatre Cedar Rapids and the Paramount Theatre. The river had reached a record high of 31.12 feet on June 13, which surpassed the 500-year flood plain. There were 1,126 city blocks that were flooded, and 561 city blocks were severely damaged. There were 7,749 properties that had been flooded and had to be evacuated (my sister and her husband being one of them). This also included 5,900 homes and 310 city facilities, some of the most notable being City Hall, Central Fire Station, the Cedar Rapids Public Library, Ground Transportation Center, Public Works building and the Animal Control building. The city of Cedar Rapids is still seeing repercussions from the Flood of 2008.

This is, by far, going to be the longest chapter in this book, as there are many locations in Cedar Rapids that are suspected to be haunted. Some of the hauntings that will be discussed have been validated with history and some are of course a folklore haunting or urban legend.

The Douglas Mansion (The History Center)

The History Center, located in the old Douglas Mansion on Eighth Street and Second Avenue southeast in Cedar Rapids, is one of the few mansions still standing on Mansion Hill.

The home was completed in 1897, and construction began in 1895. The first occupants of the home were George Bruce Douglas and his wife Irene Hazeltine Douglas.

Their eldest daughter, Margaret would also be born in 1897. Margaret would eventually marry Howard Hall, founder of Iowa Manufacturing, and they would be the last to own Brucemore Mansion.

Many people are familiar with the Douglas family for their time spent at Brucemore Mansion. The name "Brucemore" was created by George B. Douglas. Bruce is used because that is his middle name and "more" for his strong Scottish Heritage, for the "Mores of Scotland."

Douglas found his wealth within his family's businesses and industries. Douglas & Company and Quaker Oats gave the citizens of Cedar Rapids employment, which ultimately gave the Douglas Family the means to purchase and run Brucemore. Quaker Oats was George's father's cereal business. First called Douglas and Stuart, it eventually became Quaker Oats. George and his brother, Walter Douglas, pursued careers in the agribusiness industry and formed Douglas & Company and most notable Douglas Starch Works.

In 1903 George and Walter began Douglas Starch Works, which would become one of the largest cornstarch plants in the world.

In 1906, the Douglas family had grown, and they were in need of a larger home to accommodate their growing family. The widowed Caroline Sinclair was looking to downsize her home (she built Fairhome, now Brucemore). Both families had learned about each other's situation and were introduced by real estate agent Malcolm Bolton. They would execute the most memorable real estate swap in Cedar Rapids history. The Douglas family would move into Fairhome and Caroline would move into the Douglas Mansion.

Another piece of history that goes along with the Douglas Family is probably one of the most renowned tragedies in history. Walter Douglas and his wife Mahala Douglas were on a three-month trip to Europe after spending Christmas at Brucemore.

They were celebrating Walter's retirement, and purchased first-class tickets to set sail on the RMS Titanic to return home in time to celebrate Walter's birthday. They bought tickets for Mahala, her French maid and Walter. After returning to their suite, they heard the engines stop. Mahala was concerned and asked Walter to go check to see why the engines stopped. Worried, she went and put on her life preserver. They walked out to the main deck and were informed of hitting the iceberg. Mahala and her French maid were put on a lifeboat, and Mahala motioned for Walter to get on as well. He looked at her and said, "No, I must be a gentleman," and helped other women and children onto the lifeboats. Mahala and her maid would survive the tragedy, however, Walter perished among the other 1,500 passengers that went down with the ship on the early morning of April 15, 1912.

Walter's body was recovered from the wreckage by the cable ship MacKay Bennett and news got back to the Douglas family on April 23, 1912. According to the

Brucemore website, the ship's crew noted the following information, "*No. 62 - MALE - Estimated age, 55 - Hair grey, Clothing - Evening dress, with 'W.D.D.' on shirt. Effects - Gold watch; chain; gold cigarette case 'W.D.D.'; five gold studs; wedding ring on finger engraved 'May 19th '84'; pocket letter case with $551.00 and one pound; 5 note cards. First Class. Name - Walter D. Douglas, Minneapolis.*" (Brucemore, 2019).

Walter is buried in the Douglas mausoleum in Oak Hill Cemetery.

Tragedy struck Douglas Starch Works on May 22, 1919 when the factory exploded. It consumed 43 lives and caused a $2.5 million loss. There were 109 men in the plant at the time of the explosion. The explosion was so big that it could be felt 30 miles away. 10 of the 43 that were lost in the fire were not recovered. There were also 10 bodies that were partially found and they are buried in a common grave at Linwood Cemetery. There is a monument at the burial site with the encryption, "Erected In Memory of Employees of Douglas Company Who Lost Their Lives - May 22, 1919."

Robert Soutter Sinclair (son of Thomas and Caroline Sinclair) had inherited the home after his mother died and would live there until he moved him and his family to Indiana in 1923. The Turner Mortuary was looking for a larger facility since their business was a growing success. Since the Douglas Mansion was up for sale, David Turner, owner of Turner Mortuary, purchased the mansion and began renovations. Grant Wood was hired to oversee the renovations of the home and the modifications were extensive. For his efforts and oversight of the renovations, Grant was partially paid with space for a studio in the hayloft above in the carriage house. This is where he would paint the ever-so-popular "American Gothic."

The Turner Mortuary began operations in December 1924 and sold the business to the Linge family in 1978. The Linge family is known for owning and operating Cedar Memorial Cemetery, Funeral and Cremation Services. The Linge's invested to renovate the mansion back to its original look as a mansion, and funeral services stopped in 2004.

Today the Douglas Mansion is occupied by the Linn County History Center and runs and operates as a museum.

The Haunting of the Douglas Mansion

The Douglas Mansion is not open to the public for paranormal investigations. However, a local radio station, Z102.9 (KZIA) was allowed to investigate for a Halloween show. Alex Schulte and Jake Truemper (JT), were there that evening and were happy to share their experiences with us.

Alex is a little skeptical when it comes to the paranormal, but there would be experiences that night that would make him say he has witnessed the, "most substantial evidence he has ever heard."

JT is very open to the paranormal and enjoys learning more and wants to go on more investigations. Alex is even ready to go on another investigation!

Just before Halloween in 2018, Alex and JT went to the Douglas Mansion (Now the History Center) to perform the first ever investigation. They caught some incredible electronic voice phenomenon (EVP), and even a disembodied voice. They even heard a scratching noise that came from a crawl space in the music room.

The EVP they caught came from the area Elizabeth Sinclair used to call her bedroom. It is no longer there since it has been created into the museum exhibit area. It is documented that Elizabeth died in the home at 28-years-old. Elizabeth was the wife of Robert Soutter Sinclair. Elizabeth died after giving birth to their fourth child. Robert Sinclair then asked his sisters, Agnes and Amy, who were not married to move in and help raise the children and care for Caroline, who was rapidly aging.

JT was trying to communicate with Elizabeth and said, "Alright Elizabeth, we're going to go, okay?" Right after he said that they caught a young woman's voice which said, "No."

Alex and JT were near the crawl space in the music room. Alex was asking the spirits, "If you'd like us to leave please say something," and nothing was said or heard. He then asked, "If you'd like us to stay please say something." After a few seconds, a scratch is heard from that room, as if the spirits were trying to communicate to say they'd like them to stay.

The last piece of evidence that is very substantial is a disembodied voice that JT heard and caught on camera audio down in the basement next to the child crematorium burners. He was telling the spirits that they were going to be leaving soon and asked them if there is anything they want to say. Shortly after he asked, he heard a child say, "Hello." This is a disembodied voice because JT actually heard the child say that with his own ears, and they also caught it on their camera. You can tell JT heard it in the video, because he responds when he hears it by saying, "What was that? Did you just say hello?"

There have also been other claims of activity in the house from employees at the History Center. Other claims include seeing the apparition of Elizabeth Sinclair and a door slamming at the top of the stairs to a room that is no longer there (Elizabeth's Room).

Douglas Starch Works (PenFord Products / Ingredion)

As noted in the section of the Douglas Mansion, George B. Douglas and his brother Walter Douglas created Douglas Starch Works in 1903. For 16 years, Douglas Starch Works was one of the largest cornstarch plants in the world. It grew so quickly, and by 1914, it employed over 400 people. Even after the death of his brother, George kept the starch works business flourishing and expanding.

The explosion in 1919 took a toll on Douglas. He retreated to his home at Brucemore and was overcome by depression and he lived fairly quietly until his death from a cerebral hemorrhage in 1923.

In 1919, Penick & Ford, Ltd. purchased Douglas Starch Works. Eventually Penford Products would be built on top of the land where Douglas Starch Works once stood. The rebuilt plant was completed in 1921. In 1997 the companies name would change to Penford Products, and in 2014, Ingredion would buy out Penford.

The Haunting of Douglas Starch Works (Where it Once Stood)

When we were seeking out people for stories on haunted locations in the corridor, we had multiple people reach out to us and say, "What about Ingredion?' This is where Douglas Starch Works once stood, and 43 lives were lost in the tragic explosion.

Tragedy, this is one keyword in many histories to haunted locations. I'm not saying every haunting has had a tragedy, but tragic deaths are part of the recipe for a haunting and could produce the most haunted locations.

Many employees of Ingredion report creepy and eerie feelings in the tunnels. Some have even reported seeing shadow figures, or full-bodied apparitions. Ingredion is a secure location that will not allow access to those who do not work there, due to safety reasons.

Oak Hill Cemetery

Oak Hill Cemetery is home to many iconic Cedar Rapidians. It is one of the oldest cemeteries in Linn County. It is the final resting place for many of the Douglas Family members, Howard and Margaret Hall, The Sinclair family and many other prominent philanthropists of Cedar Rapids.

In 1852, the land development to the east was overtaking the small Village, also known as Washington Cemetery. This was located at 8th Street and 5th Avenue Southeast. Relocation of these graves was necessary, and they were moved to the new Oak Hill Cemetery in 1856. The Oak Hill Cemetery was first run as a for-profit cemetery and not long after its development it was reorganized as the Oak Hill Cemetery Association and switched to a non-profit organization.

This photo is of the Sinclair Family plot.

The entrance of the cemetery was installed in 1908, and the receiving vault was used near the entrance until 1918.

The cemetery was added to the National Register of Historic Places in May 2013. Some notable families buried in Oak Hill Cemetery are the Douglas Family, Hall Family, Sinclair Family, Dows Family and the Ely Family, just to name a few.

The Urban Legend of Tillie at Oak Hill Cemetery

In the Oak Hill Cemetery Association's newsletter in fall 2007, they address the alleged spirit of Tillie. They state that an internet search will reveal similar accounts with Tillie. However, no one can say they have actually "seen" Tillie.

The legend of Tillie is as follows, *"A Czech girl haunts this graveyard carrying a flickering candle and trying to pull people into one of the mausoleums. She is buried in the potter's field section of the cemetery."*

Later on, in this newsletter they state that the potter's field portion of the cemetery does not exist in Oak Hill

Cemetery. It was part of the City Cemetery that was maintained by the City Parks Department. Stories of Tillie date back to the 1960s and they started when one of the cemetery workers created her story to scare a co-worker. Another discrepancy is that no mausoleums exist in the section of the cemetery that is known as City Cemetery.

I remember hearing stories of Tillie when I was a little girl. I would never want to go into the cemetery because of this. Young and naïve I didn't realize that it was just an urban legend.

Now, could Tillie be a tulpa by now? I believe she could. However, the association does make a point to remind everyone that a cemetery is a testament to the memory of the people who lived and are now buried there.

Please remember to respect those who have passed and their final resting places.

Old Cedar Rapids Public Library

Many will know the location of the old Cedar Rapids Public Library. However, out of respect for the current business that occupies the building, I am going to leave out the address and the name of the business.

The history of the old public library does not go very far back. The doors opened in February 1985. So, one would wonder why it is haunted. Or is it haunted?

Urban Legends and Folklore Haunting's of the Cedar Rapids Public Library

In 2008, the old public library suffered major flood damage. Before the flood, many stated that they had seen the apparition of an elderly woman walking through the aisles of the books. A frequent visitor of the library was an elderly woman; I am going to leave her name out of the story, out of respect for the family. One day, staff learned of her death and not long after claimed to see her roaming through the aisles of the library. In addition to seeing her, many claimed to see books flying off the shelves.

Coe College

Coe College sits just outside of Downtown Cedar Rapids off of First Avenue. According to the college's website, "Coe College claims the shortest name of any American institution of higher education, but the school has actually carried five titles through its history," (Coe College, 2019).

The college was founded in 1851 as The School for the Prophets by Rev. Williston Jones. He was the first resident minister in Cedar Rapids and opened the parlor of his home to a group of young men. The goal was to educate them for the ministry to serve churches in the Midwest (Coe College, 2019).

In 1853 Jones was busy seeking out churches in the East for money to send three of his students to seminaries in the East. Daniel Coe, a Catskills farmer came forward and pledged $1,500 and insisted that Jones start his own college in Cedar Rapids. Coe had a stipulation with his pledge though, he said that the college should be "made available for the education of females as well as males," (Coe College, 2019). This made Coe College a coeducational institution from its beginnings.

In 1853, the Cedar Rapids Collegiate Institute was incorporated by a group of Cedar Rapids leaders (Coe College, 2019). This group was led by Judge George Greene. The $1,500 pledged by Coe was used to purchase 80 acres of farmland for the school, which was just on the edge of town. This would eventually become the campus you see today.

In 1868, the school underwent yet another name change. It was changed to Parsons Seminary, in a not-so-successful event in trying to secure Lewis Parsons estate. The college went through some severe financial difficulties and it was reestablished as Coe Collegiate Institute in honor of the original donor, Daniel Coe (Coe College, 2019).

Prominent figures in Cedar Rapids contributed to the financial stability of Coe College in its infancy. T. M Sinclair, who founded Sinclair Meat Packing Company, played a huge role in financially in the final steps towards the establishment of Coe College. His gift liquidated all of the debt from the Parsons Seminary and the Cedar Rapids Collegiate Institute (Coe College, 2019). It made it practical for the land of the Coe Collegiate Institute, which included the original land funded by Daniel Coe, to be transferred to Coe College (Coe College, 2019). The institute was run by the Iowa Presbyterian Synod. Since February 2, 1881, Coe College has been operating continuously.

Photo is the Sinclair Memorial Chapel on the Coe College Campus

Many building projects commenced over the years. According to the Coe College website, these buildings included Old Main (1868), Williston Hall (1881), Marshall Hall (1900), the first gymnasium (1904), and the first T.M. Sinclair Memorial Chapel (1911) (Coe College, 2019).

Coe College earned accreditation from the North Central Association of Colleges and Universities in 1907 (Coe College, 2019). Its reputation is considered as a superior liberal arts college and continues to grow.

Voorhees Hall

Voorhees Hall is one of the oldest buildings on the Coe College campus. It is well-known for the ghost of Helen Roberts. The construction of Voorhees Hall was made possible by Ralph and Elizabeth Voorhees in 1914.

They also contributed a library, chapel and endowment gift to Rutgers University.

Voorhees hall was set to be a state-of-the-art facility for women. There were singles and doubles for women, and the first floor included two apartments for college guests and a few suite rooms (Coe College, 2019). There was an infirmary on the third floor, which included two large rooms and a bathroom for women who were ill. The infirmary would become a hotspot for the women in 1918 with the Spanish influenza epidemic.

One of the women who passed away in the infirmary would become well-known throughout the city of Cedar Rapids, and still is known in the present day.

The Ghost Story of Helen Roberts in Voorhees Hall

Helen Roberts died in the infirmary from complications with Spanish influenza, where she contracted pneumonia. She died on October 19, 1918. Some say she still lingers throughout Voorhees Hall since she was cut short of her college experience and is now trying to live out her college days.

Helen was a freshman from Strawberry Point, Iowa. She had begun at Coe College just three weeks before she was overcome with the Spanish influenza (Keenan, 2018). Coe College professor Dr. Charles T. Hickok and his wife attended her funeral in Strawberry Point. Her parents wanted her legacy to continue at Coe College, so they donated a grandfather clock to Voorhees Hall (Keenan, 2018). This clock can still be seen in Voorhees Hall today.

There are many students that claim they still can see and feel the spirit of Helen today. The ghost stories of Helen began in the 70s and have continued ever since. I'm sure some stories have been embellished, and "over done," but there is no doubt that Helen could still be roaming the corridors of Voorhees Hall.

Some of the sightings of Helen include seeing her near the grandfather clock, and a cold breeze next to it. Also, some claim they have received a phantom phone call and on the other end is a woman who has a very weak voice. Some women claim they are locked out of their rooms, and that Helen does not like it when male visitors come to Voorhees Hall. Helen was a part of Delta Delta Delta, and they claim they get the most activity and experiences with Helen. Helen is never mean or vindictive. She is a very friendly spirit, and just wants to continue on her college days that she never got to live out.

We were fortunate enough to be able to get some firsthand stories from previous residents of Voorhees Hall. Morgan J. East lived in Voorhees Hall a few times while attending Coe College. She also reminisced about her mother having some stories about Helen when her mother attended Coe.

Morgan told us about when her mom attended Coe, they had a "Helen Cam" setup that pointed at the clock and people watching could essentially screenshot images of Helen. She isn't sure if anyone caught her on camera or not. Morgan said she was always a little hesitant to live in Voorhees Hall knowing the history of it and the claims of it being haunted by Helen. She lived in Voorhees a few different years and in a couple of different areas of the dormitory.

When she first moved in, she set her alarm for the same time every day, but there was one week that it would go off at random times during the night. In that same room she was sitting online playing euchre and her fridge was over by the door with her microwave on top of it, she had some silverware and plates she needed to wash that was also sitting on top of the fridge. She heard the silverware rattle, thinking it was just the fridge making it shake. She didn't pay much attention to it and kept playing euchre. The next thing that happened was she heard a piece of silverware hit the wall and a spoon had gone from one side of the room to the other on its own. Morgan had lived in a single room at the time, so it wasn't very wide, but it was a far enough distance that it frightened her quite a bit, and she left her dorm for a while. This is just the beginning of her experiences with

Helen. The experience with the alarm and the spoon flying across the room happened within about two months of living in the dorm.

Her boyfriend at the time also had experiences in her dorm room. If you remember from before, it was said that Helen didn't necessarily care for male visitors, and she would definitely let it be known. Morgan was sleeping on her loft bed and her boyfriend was on the floor. She couldn't sleep that night, and all of the sudden she felt something pushing down on her on the bed. She knew it wasn't sleep paralysis, because she had been moving around just seconds before she felt the pressure on her. She felt a pressure on her left shoulder for a minute or so. Once the pressure lifted, there was a shelf she had on her dresser and it fell over and woke her boyfriend up. She told him what had happened, and she couldn't sleep the rest of the night. That was about the end of the activity in that room. The next academic year she moved into the room that was across the hall. She lived on first west, which was the floor right under the Tri-Delta wing.

In her second year in Voorhees Hall, she had similar experiences with silverware. That was about it for that room, and then she moved into third floor east.

She states she can't count how many times her television and stereo turned on and off by itself at any time of the day. Morgan even at one point could hear typing sounds coming from her laptop when she'd be lying up in bed. This also happened to one of her friends who lived on the first floor. She had a few friends who would try and trigger Helen to be active, and as soon as they would, she would start to do things. The television would turn on and start changing channels. Morgan would even wake up in the middle of the night to what seemed to be someone shaking her pillows. She also had another incident where she felt like she was being touched. However, the most common occurrences were electronics being manipulated. She stated that this would be a couple times a month, or even sometimes a couple times a week.

Morgan went on to tell us that she heard if you lived in Helen's room, she didn't like things being put up on the wall. Many claimed they would have posters and things taken down, or when trying to put posters up on the wall, they could not get them to stick. She said they tried about every method to get them up on the wall.

JOSH AND KATIE HOPKINS

CHAPTER 9

THE OUTSKIRTS

This chapter is going to include haunted locations that are not in the corridor, but just outside of it (within 90 miles). This chapter will include locations from Cedar Falls, Iowa, Strawberry Point, Iowa and Rock Island, Illinois.

Cedar Falls, Iowa

The city of Cedar Falls is just a little over 60 miles northwest of Cedar Rapids. In its early years it was known as Sturgis Falls, after William Sturgis and his brother-in-law Erasmus Adams were the first permanent residents in the area.

They were brought to the area because of their fascination with the farm land, timber and the Cedar River. They sold the community to John and Dempsey Overman, as well as, John Barrick in 1850 and they renamed the town Cedar Falls. Overman Park in Cedar Falls is named after John and Dempsey Overman.

From 1855 to 1860 Cedar Falls grew from around 450 to more than 1,500 people, and the area began to develop and thrive. The first post office was created in 1850, the schoolhouse in 1853 and the railroad connection in 1861.

Businesses were booming in Cedar Falls, some that are still apparent today. These include, Viking Pump and Sartori Hospital. Others that are no longer around are The Broom Factory and the Cedar Falls Bible Conference.

The City of Cedar Falls had one of the fastest population growths in the state from 1950-1980.

The smallest of Iowa's state schools, The University of Northern Iowa, is located in Cedar Falls. This is where Katie would attend college for her undergraduate degree.

The population of Cedar Falls in 2017 was 41,570 people.

University of Northern Iowa

The University of Northern Iowa (UNI) has a deep rich history that dates back to the mid-1800s. One of the most notable pieces of history is the Civil War Orphanage that was located on campus in 1866. This orphanage was founded by Annie Turner Wittenmeyer, and a memorial to her and the orphanage can be found outside of Lang Hall to this day. Once the orphans grew up and were moving out of the orphanage there was no need any more for the orphanage. This created the Iowa State Normal School in 1876. The school was dedicated to the training of teachers. The university has gone through a few name changes before landing on UNI. It was first the Iowa State Normal School, then Iowa State

Teachers College, State College of Iowa and most recently the University of Northern Iowa. In the 2017 fall term there was 11,907 students enrolled. It is the smallest of the state schools in Iowa.

Bartlett Hall

Enrollment at the Iowa Normal School was rapidly increasing and by 1892 the school needed more classroom space and that resulted in them closing the on-campus housing. Students had to find a place to live either in rooming houses or at home. Ultimately the closing of the Boarding Department led to the creation of the College Hill neighborhood (Witthoft, 1996). Many of the large houses were built just before or right at the turn of the century. This provided rooming and boarding for the college students.

With the adequate rooming situations, inspected by Dean of Women Marion McFarland Walker, many students were able to find places to live while attending school. However, many school officials were still leery of the living situations for students, because they felt they needed more control over the students' lives since a majority of the students enrolled were women (Witthoft, 1996). This led to President Seerly asking the General Assembly to fund a women's dormitory in 1912 (Witthoft, 1996). The General Assembly accepted and approved $100,000 to fund the dormitory in 1913. Plans were drawn up by W.T. Proudfoot in March 1914. The dormitory would be located on the north edge of the college campus (Witthoft, 1996). The dormitory would house approximately 150 women and would have a cafeteria. The response by women to want to live in the dormitory was outstanding. This encouraged the Board to request two additional wings to the building to accommodate the women.

Photo Courtesy of Rod Library, The University of Northern Iowa

The campus was thriving and the buildings on campus were becoming abundant. According to Witthoft, "the old geographical names – North Hall, South Hall and Central Hall – no longer served a useful purpose," (1996). This encouraged President Seerly to propose the name of the dormitory be changed. He asked that it be named in honor of Moses Willard Bartlett, who was a faculty member of the first faculty of the Iowa Normal School in 1876. He was a mathematics professor from 1876-1881 and an English language and literature professor from 1881 until he retired in 1904 (Witthoft, 1996). In addition, he was the Assistant Principal of Normal School from 1880-1888. Bartlett Hall was one of the first buildings on campus, along with Old Gilchrist Hall, to be named after something other than a geographical name (Witthoft, 1996).

In June 1914, the construction of the first unit began. I want to mention, this is the unit I lived in while I was at UNI, I only lived there my freshman year. On September 13, 1915, students moved into the dorm. Unit one had sixty-two double occupancy rooms and a large reception room (Witthoft, 1996). The cafeteria opened a day later on September 14, 1915.

The second unit was completed in 1916 and had a larger dining room (Witthoft, 1996). The third unit was completed in 1924 and cost about $160,000 (Witthoft, 1996). It accommodated around two hundred more women. Short presentations were done by Pauline Lewelling Devitt and Anna B. Lawther (a name you will hear again when we discuss Lawther Hall). They were both members of the Board of Education.

In total, the construction of Bartlett Hall cost $475,000 (Witthoft, 1996). Bartlett Hall provided housing for over 510 women.

In 1942, after the fall term the college was contracted to provide housing, facilities and training to the U.S. Navy and the Army Air Corps in regard to World War II war efforts (Witthoft, 1996). The women in Bartlett Hall moved out to accommodate for a thousand WAVES. From 1942 to early 1945 Bartlett Hall housed women who were in WAVES boot camp and yeoman training (Witthoft, 1996). The dining area that used to be located on the ground floor became the sick bay and the color scheme became military. Once the WAVES left on April 30, 1945, they redecorated the entire hall once again.

Halloween was brought to UNI as early as the late 1800s. Many students held their own Halloween parties in their dorm rooms. Their parities included pumpkin carving, taffy pulls, and games. By 1910, many university organizations were hosting their own parties. Bartlett Hall hosted a Halloween Dinner in 1933, and in 1935 their Halloween party consisted of a dance and other activities.

In the spring of 2012, the decision was made to no longer have Bartlett Hall as a residence hall. As the university was tearing down Baker Hall, which housed multiple faculty offices, they moved them into Bartlett Hall in 2013.

Bartlett Hall served as a wonderful housing unit for many students for 97 years.

Katie's Time in Bartlett Hall

In May 2005, I graduated from high school, and it was time to start thinking about moving away from home in August for college. I knew Bartlett Hall was going to be tough to get into since it was the only dormitory with air condition, so *everyone* wanted to live there. I want to note, Bartlett Hall was no longer just a women's dorm, and there were certain halls that had men living in them now. I have pretty bad asthma, and I put that in my application to live there, since in the summer the allergens in the air tend to spike my asthma and I have trouble breathing. I received my housing information and I was accepted into Bartlett Hall!

It was mid-August 2005 and I made the hour and a half drive from Walford, with my parents following, to move into my dorm room. I lived in a double occupancy room with a roommate that I did not know. I eventually ended up moving into a different room at the end of the fall semester, as I had befriended my neighbor, who is still my best friend to this day.

I didn't have many experiences in my first dorm room. It was when I moved into unit one of Bartlett Hall (the oldest portion of Bartlett Hall) that I started to experience activity.

Typically, on weekends I would go home to Walford, and do laundry and see my family. I got homesick pretty easily, so I liked to go home and see my family. However, there were a few weekends where I stayed in Cedar Falls, and it just so happened those weekends I stayed, my friend would go home. Every night that I would be alone in the dorm room, I could not sleep and I had to have the television on all night to help me sleep. I also wouldn't sleep on my bunk; I would sleep on the futon. I am not sure why, but I felt more comfortable on the futon, even though the bars would dig into my back. For some reason though, I always slept better on the futon.

One day, I had gone down to the restroom, and when I got back the faucet was on in our room. I thought to myself, oh my friend must be back and left the water on. I text her and asked her where she was, and she responded, "still at home." Well, this was alarming. I know I locked the door when I went to the restroom, so no one could have gotten in to my room to turn the water on. More importantly, why would anyone do that? I knew though that no one had gotten in my dorm room because I had to unlock it to get back in coming back from the restroom. I shut the water off, in confusion, and just went about my day. It was still daylight so that at least was nice to ease the fear.

It quickly became time to go to bed, I figured I would try and sleep in my bunk as it was more comfortable than the futon (physically). I got up in bed, and immediately felt uneasy. I felt like "all eyes were on me." I didn't even want to look out from under my covers thinking I would see someone standing there. I turned on my light, got down from my bunk, turned on the television and made a bed on the futon. I always turned on Disney Channel because I knew they didn't play scary movie trailers. I sat there and watched the Disney Channel for hours before becoming tired enough to just fall asleep.

Finally, there was sunlight coming through the window. I was so thankful that it was morning and I went to the Rialto (cafeteria in the Towers) to get breakfast. I took my breakfast back to my dorm as I didn't want to eat by myself in the cafeteria. I sat on my computer and was scoping out Facebook. This is the Facebook before you could message people, you could only write on their wall. I couldn't wait until my friend got back so I didn't have to be alone in the dorm room.

That is the experience that sticks out to me the most from my time in Bartlett Hall. I did have small occurrences throughout the academic year that I lived there. I would hear voices (in my room, not outside in the hallway), and the most notable was always the eerie feeling and feeling like there was always eyes on me.

May 2006 came, and I ended up moving back to Cedar Rapids, as I decided I better go to community college before committing to a university. I was happy to move home after living in Bartlett Hall. However, I will always be thankful for my time at Bartlett Hall because it brought me to one of my dearest friends.

Urban Legends of Bartlett Hall

One of the biggest misconceptions of Bartlett Hall is that it was used as an infirmary on the third floor. This is not true; the infirmary was actually on the third floor of Lawther Hall which is connected to Bartlett Hall by The Commons area.

So, with this urban legend, people have claimed they see soldiers and hear the hustle and bustle of an infirmary. There really is not much to share about urban legends of Bartlett Hall as many of the claims and stories of a ghost seem to be true, and general.

The Haunting of Bartlett Hall – Claims from Residents/Students

It is said that students tried to revive the Halloween Haunted House on the third floor for many years. However, it never took place because students would be scared out of the third floor by the actual ghosts who haunt Bartlett Hall. They stated that during the setup they would get many eerie feelings. Lights would flicker, doors would slam, temperature would drastically change, and eventually this led to students giving up on their efforts to create a haunted house.

Many previous residents make the same claims as I have experienced. Lights flickering, their sink turned on and off by itself, feeling uneasy, feeling of being watched.

It does make me wonder, with Bartlett Hall being changed from a residence hall to offices, if that has triggered more activity or if it has ceased with the change of environment.

Lawther Hall

By the end of the 1930s, enrollment and need for more housing units was needed. Bartlett Hall had been filled to its capacity with 520 women and many women were being turned away because there were no housing units for them to live in. In July 1938, plans were in place to start building a new women's dormitory (Witthoft & Peterson, 1996). Lawther Hall would be built west of the Commons and be similar to Bartlett Hall.

In the summer of 1940, the "Addition to Bartlett Hall" was opened to 293 women. In June 1940, President Latham made the decision that the hall would be named after Anna B. Lawther and gave it the name Lawther Hall (Witthoft & Peterson, 1996).

Photo Courtesy of Rod Library, The University of Northern Iowa

Anna B. Lawther was the first woman voted to the State Board of Education (Witthoft & Peterson, 1996). She was served for twenty years starting in 1921.

Many of the women living in Bartlett Hall were moved to Lawther Hall when the WAVES came in during World War II.

Lawther Hall is still a housing facility on the campus at UNI. It is located on West 23rd Street.

The Urban Legend of "Augie"

The only reason I put this under urban legends is because it has not been validated with actual historical documents that an Augie lived or was in the infirmary at Lawther Hall. I am not saying Augie doesn't exist, but with no documentation of him, I cannot say he has been validated.

Many ghost stories have circulated about Lawther Hall over the years. The legend began when people started saying they were seeing Augie in Lawther Hall. They believe that Augie is a WWII soldier, who died in Lawther Hall when it was an infirmary. This has not been confirmed.

It is said that Augie was first seen up in the attic of Lawther Hall, but recently has been seen throughout the housing facility.

The first reports of Augie were mentioned in the student newspaper in 1977. The claim was that he had changed the lettering on a bulletin board outside one of the rooms to say, "Augie will return to haunt Bordeaux House."

More reports of Augie were seen in 1992 when a resident assistant claimed they saw a man in a striped outfit walking down the hall and then went into the women's bathroom. They ran into the bathroom and no one was there. He is also said to take posters off of walls and place them on the floor. Many women reported that they would wake up and a poster would be in the middle of their dorm room, on the floor. It is also said he would turn on radios and that the radio would get unplugged and still continue to play. He is also reported to have turned on water in the middle of the night (hmmm sounds familiar!). It is said that Augie has been reported many times being seen in his military uniform.

In 1999, two residents of Lawther Hall reported that they were sitting in the hallway and all the sudden felt something walk through their legs. They also, in addition to this, heard footsteps. This was at 3:00 AM. It is also reported that some would see Augie's face on the ceiling just before turning lights on or off.

One of the most unnerving stories about Augie is from a resident that was getting ready for bed, and the television screen went blue. The resident could hear footsteps dragging across the floor and all of the sudden felt someone tugging her sheets from the end of the bed. She had to hold so tightly that when the tugging stopped, she punched herself in the face. She stated that the television screen then flickered and had "good night" written across it.

In the 1970s there was a private investigator hired to investigate the happenings going on in Lawther Hall. The experiences were documented and reported on IPBN's show "Take One" in October 1985.

I tried to find records of Augie and was unsuccessful.

Lang Hall

Lang Hall has been on the UNI campus since 1900. It is the oldest surviving instructional building on campus (Wittenhoft & Grant, 1996). It is most well-known as the Auditorium Building. It was named after William C. Lang in September 1994 (Wittenhoft & Grant, 1996). Lang was a professor from 1949 through 1978. He first taught history and was the Head of the Social Science Department from 1955-1959 (Wittenhoft & Grant, 1996). He eventually took on the roles of Dean of the College, Dean of Instruction and eventually the Vice President of Academic Affairs (Wittenhoft & Grant, 1996). He resigned from that position and taught history again until he retired in 1978. Once retired, he co-authored a two-volume centennial history of UNI, titled *A Century of Leadership and Service* (Wittenhoft & Grant, 1996).

Photo Courtesy of Rod Library, The University of Northern Iowa

In May 1995, a formal dedication took place in the auditorium to honor Professor Lang (Wittenhoft & Grant, 1996).

In Lang Hall you will find bas-relief reproductions of commemorative plaque from the Soldiers and Sailors Monument in Des Moines. These are Civil War based plaques.

113

In 1900, construction commenced on Lang Hall and in 1901, 18 rooms were ready for instruction. The Auditorium Building was completed by December 1901 (Wittenhoft & Grant, 1996).

Lang Hall has three floors and a basement. In which I have had classes on all floors of that building. In its infancy it had a gymnasium, fifty classrooms, and literary society halls (Wittenhoft & Grant, 1996). Most recently Lang Hall housed multiple Liberal Arts courses and Public Relations classes. I had both liberal arts and public relations courses in Lang Hall.

A "tunnel" was created to connect Lang Hall and the Union. The Union is a common area with a food court and area for students to study and hang out with friends.

Annie Turner Wittenmyer (Civil War Orphanage)

When you visit Lang Hall, the entrance off College Street, has a remarkable statue out front. This statue is in honor and in memory of Annie Tuner Wittenmyer.

Annie Turner Wittenmyer was a Civil War relief effort activist. She was born on August 26, 1827 near Sandy Springs, Adams County, Ohio, and was the eldest daughter of John G and Elizabeth Turner. In 1847, she married William Wittenmyer. He was a wealthy merchant from Jacksonville, Ohio. In 1850, they moved to Keokuk, Iowa. This is where Annie would become involved in civic affairs. She is responsible for opening a free school, which was largely attended by the children of the community's poor families, in 1853.

She was a little thrown back by the lack of religious and moral training in the area so she opened up a Sunday school.

With the Civil War on the horizons, Keokuk was a major point for the deployment of Iowa soldiers. This encouraged many women of Keokuk to create the Ladies' Soldiers' Aid Society. Annie was the secretary and general agent of the organization.

Annie's husband and three of her four children had passed away before the Civil War, so she spent much of her time working with the troops. She put most of her effort in medical aspects and taking care of injured soldiers. This opened her eyes to many horrors of war, and one of those being children losing their families.

She created the Iowa Soldiers' Orphans' Home Association in the fall of 1863. The association transferred to the state of Iowa in 1866. This established orphanages in Davenport, Cedar Falls, and Glenwood. The Cedar Falls and Glenwood sites would close in the 1870's. The site in Cedar Falls would eventually become the Iowa State Normal School.

In 1868, Annie moved to Philadelphia, Pennsylvania after being invited by Bishop Matthew Simpson to establish women's work within the Methodist Episcopal Church. She would never return to Iowa.

On February 2, 1900, Annie passed away at her home in Sanatoga, Pennsylvania.

Her memorial at the UNI commemorates the many achievements she had during her lifetime. On the memorial, there are seven tablets that are engraved with her achievements. At the top of the memorial is a bronze contemporary reinterpretation of the victorious Nike (Winged Victory). This symbolizes her triumph over social injustice and war.

Where Lang Hall stands today is where the orphanage would have been located.

The Urban Legend of "Zelda"

The auditorium in the basement of Lang Hall is suspected to be haunted by the ghost of Zelda. Zelda is known to go between Lang Hall and Strayer-Wood Theatre since she is a "theatrical" ghost. Her origins are unknown, but some say it could possibly be an old professor from the Normal School. The folklore is that the professor either died in class or on stage, or it was someone nearby who wanted to go to the Normal School but ended up passing away.

Those who claim to have experiences with Zelda say she was often seen in the main hallway and staircase that passes in front of the auditorium, late at night. Many say she likes to play tricks on people, and will shut lights off, yelling insults, opening and closing doors, and playing piano.

I had class on each floor of Lang Hall. Many do get the misconception that the orphanage was Lang Hall, but in fact, it was not. The orphanage or to the Iowa State Normal School, was Central Hall. Central Hall stood about where Mauker Union is today. Central Hall burnt down on July 22, 1965. The fire was believed to happen to do a faulty wire.

My experiences in Lang Hall were minimal, but both my sister Emily and I, always felt like we were being watched and got creepy feelings in Lang Hall. Especially in the auditorium and in the basement. This would be the closest areas to Mauker Union and where Central Hall would have been located.

Strawberry Point

A little over 60 miles north of Cedar Rapids, is the small town of Strawberry Point. Strawberry Point has been around since Iowa was just a territory in 1841. Strawberry Point was considered one of the areas as "Neutral Ground", which was a barrier to protect Indians from Indians. More specifically, the Winnebagos and the hostile tribes (Sac and Fox Tribes). "Old Mission Road" went from Strawberry Point to Fort Atkinson (and there were other "Old Mission Road" tracks), it was basically a military wagon road. Fort Atkinson is where they gave shelter and safety to Indians who were trying to get away from hostile tribes.

In 1853 the town of Strawberry Point was laid out and was first recorded on a plat map in 1854.

Strawberry Point was known as the "Cream City" in 1887 due to receiving 10,731,428 gallons of whole milk, which made Strawberry Point one of the top locations for processing whole milk.

The population reported in 2017 was 1,233 people.

Franklin Hotel

The Franklin Hotel sits on a corner lot that dates back to 1854. G.I. Termaine and his brother-in-law Alex Blake constructed a wood frame building in 1854 on the corner lot, where the Franklin Hotel stands today. Eventually Termaine sold his interest in the house to Blake. Blake renamed it the Blake House and in 1902 he sold it to the Franklin Hotel and Land Company. They demolished the old wooden structure and built a new brick hotel.

In 1902, the Franklin Hotel would come alive and much of what you see today is original from 1902.

The Haunting of the Franklin Hotel

It is hard to say whether or not the suspected ghost of the Franklin Hotel actually existed. However, there are many run-ins with the ghost of the old hotel. According to the Franklin Hotel website, they state that the ghost is allegedly a prostitute who stayed there in the 1920s.

The first claims of a haunting are from a couple who stayed at the hotel and felt the prostitute's presence. They both said that the energy from the presence felt upset, and that it was because the mirror that had once been there was moved. This mirror was said to be her favorite fixture in that room.

Many people who stay in the hotel claim they hear noises that cannot be explained. The owner has also said that he has seen a woman in a lavender gown. She walked from the lobby to the dining room, and when he went to go tell her they were closed, he couldn't find her.

According to the Franklin Hotel's website, the owner did not believe in ghosts, and then he saw the Lady in Lavender.

Elkader

Elkader is just northeast of Strawberry Point, and about 78 miles northeast of Cedar Rapids.

Elkader began as Pony Hollow in 1836 when the first residents arrived. Elisha Boardman and Horace Bronson settled there and Boardman created the first farm and with the help of other early settlers established the first school house. On June 22, 1846, the land was officially platted by Timothy Davis, John Thompson and Chester Sage. Davis was in charge of coming up with a name for the new village, and chose Elkader after Abd el-Kader. El-Kader in 1830-1847 led his people in a resistance to French Colonialism.

By 1847, the first retail store, sawmill and gristmill were in operation. In addition, a blacksmith arrived in the village and Elkader was the focal point for local activity.

In 1849, Elkader unsuccessfully bid to be the county seat of Clayton County. They lost to Garnavillo. However, in 1859 with a growing population, a foundry, a wagon and carriage shop, plow shop and other new businesses, Elkader bid again and won. With other votes between 1864-1868, the county seat had changed a few times. It again became the county seat in 1868, and remains the county seat today.

The population in 2017 of Elkader was 1,226.

Lover's Leap

The history of Lover's Leap is very unique and quite the love story. It is almost a 19th Century Romeo and Juliet. In 1831, the Millville family lived north of Dubuque. Lou, the son, befriended the neighboring Indians, and he was even "friendlier" with the Indian Chief, Grey Eagle's daughter, who was White Cloud.

Lou was aware of a lead mine that the Indian's had just a short distance from Dubuque. Against White Cloud's wishes, he followed two braves into the forest to learn the secret of the mines. He was eventually discovered and captured by the Indians. The next morning at dawn, he was ordered to jump from the cliff into the water. He stood ready to jump, but instead he turned and leaped at his captors and attacked them. He eventually was tomahawked and lost consciousness, but not before he threw his attackers over the cliff.

Still unconscious by the cliff, White Cloud found him and thought he had perished. She had followed him in her canoe to watch for his safety. She found him lying there, removed her moccasins and jumped over the side of the cliff to her death. Once Lou had come to and gained consciousness again, he found her moccasins lying next to him.

He looked over the side of the cliff and saw her lifeless body lying there on the rocks by the water. He gathered her body and buried it on the cliff from where she had jumped.

The legend says that Lou had visited her grave yearly up until his death, which eventually gave the cliff the name "Lover's Leap".

The Urban Legend of Lover's Leap

Many claim to come across the ghost of White Cloud when they visit Lover's Leap. Even though there is a complete story to Lover's Leap, it was never documented, and it is unknown if White Cloud is actually buried there.

Other claims include hearing screaming as if someone has just jumped from the cliff, and also seeing a young man walking around the cliff (possibly Lou coming to White Cloud's grave)? Another involves hearing what sounds to be a struggle or fight. This could possibly be Lou fighting off his attackers and throwing them over the cliff.

Hopkinton, Iowa

Hopkinton was discovered and laid out in 1850 and was incorporated in 1874. It is a small town in Delaware County. The population in 2017 was only 601 people.

There is not much to be found about Hopkinton, Iowa when researching. Much of the research brings up notable people and of course Lenox College.

Some of the first settlers near Hopkinton were James and Hugh Livingston and Hugh Rose. They came from Selkirk Colony in Northern Canada, and eventually ended up in Scotch Grove, Iowa in Jones County. They eventually settled just a short distance south of the town of Hopkinton. They became a great influence in the area and improved farmland and became great men of the church and community.

Hugh Livingston would become a physician and surgeon in Hopkinton and attended three years at Lenox College.

Lenox College

Lenox College was in operation from 1859 to 1944. It was originally known as Bowen Collegiate Institute, and the name was changed to Lenox Collegiate Institute in October 1864 and Lenox College in 1884.

It was associated with the Presbyterian Church and several of the buildings on the campus are part of the National Register of Historic Places.

The Old Main building was constructed in 1856. It is Victorian style architecture and the east wing was added in 1875. Clarke Hall which was the dormitory for women was built in 1890 and Doolittle Hall was built in 1900. Doolittle hall had a library and literary societies. The gym, which is Finkbonner Hall was built in 1916.

There is a Civil War Monument located in the center of the college campus. It was dedicated on November 17, 1865. It was the first monument on the campus that was dedicated to the Civil War. Many of the male students and the Dean of the College enlisted into military service soon after the war began. This caused the school to close temporarily, and the monument is dedicated to them.

The first President of the college was Dr. W.L. Roberts and he was elected as president on December 12, 1859.

Some notable alumni are Samuel Calvin (1840-1911), pioneering Iowa geologist and professor at the University of Iowa, Thomas Macbride (1848–1934), president at University of Iowa (1914-1916), and Mary Walker (1832-1919), American feminist, abolitionist, prohibitionist, alleged spy, prisoner of war and surgeon. She is the only woman ever to receive the Medal of Honor.

The Urban Legend of Lenox College

Some have said that they have seen a woman in one of the dormitory hall windows. The story is that she is waiting for her fiancé to return from the war. A family was walking by one of the dorms and a little girl asked, "Do you see her? The lady in the window!" When everyone else looked, there was no one there.

We are considering this an urban legend as no one has been able to verify this happened. We are not saying it didn't happen, and the history adds up, but at this point in time it is still a legend.

Rock Island, Illinois (Quad Cities)

Just a little over 85 miles southeast of Cedar Rapids is the city of Rock Island, Illinois. Known for the Rock Island Arsenal and the Rock Island Railway, it is part of the community of the Quad Cities.

History of Rock Island dates back to 1835. Black Hawk was as Sauk Warrior who lived in Rock Island when the United States Army secured the upper Mississippi for white settlers. The creation of Fort Armstrong (which is now Rock Island) served as a military post to attract more white settlers and it is ultimately what led to the fall of the Black Hawk Indians in the area. It pushed the Sauk and Fox Indian tribes to move west.

Rock Island was given its name in 1841 from previously being named Fort Armstrong.

The railway brought a lot of prosperity to the area and its industries. In 1856, when Chicago and Rock Island built the railroad, and built the first railroad bridge, it allowed for many supplies to be transferred from a long distance.

Needless to say, there has been a lot of industry and a lot of people to pass through the city of Rock Island.

In 2017, the population of Rock Island was 38,110 people.

The Rock Island YMCA (D. Vinar Furniture)

The Rock Island YMCA was built in 1912 and opened its doors in 1913. Many railroad workers, military personnel, and men would stop here if they needed a place to stay. It was mentioned that in the early days of the YMCA, some of the locations were disguises for speakeasy's and brothels. Many dances were held on the main floor.

The Haunting of and the Unknown Darkness Investigation of the Old Rock Island YMCA

The Unknown Darkness team was invited to tag along on a paranormal investigation on March 16, 2019. We arrived at the location around 5:45 PM and were given a tour of the old building.

We started on the main floor, and first worked our way down to the old pool area. Once you get into the old pool area, you can look up and see the old running track.

The area where the pool once was goes deep within the basement of the building. Now, it is inhabited by multiple storage units, artifacts and furniture. You can still see remnants of the pool tile. The deeper you go within the basement, the heavier the energy. It is documented that a little boy drowned in the pool.

We were back in one of the storage areas, and it just felt like multiple spirits were coming out from behind the shelves and artifacts. It was so dark; you couldn't even see your hand right in front of your face.

After the rush of energy, we weren't feeling much anymore in the basement, so we decided to go upstairs to the fourth floor. The fourth floor, the folklore haunting is that a woman was assaulted in the shower room. This is not documented, and it was a claim from a medium that visited there. So, this can only be documented as folklore or an urban legend. We didn't get much in the shower room. It was outside of the shower room in the hallway that we would feel and see the most energy.

One of the investigators that was tagging along with us from a different team had an ancient Japanese Singing Bowl. They started to make the singing bowl, sing. A singing bowl is used to emanate spirit activity through sound. A singing bowl induces clarity of the mind, and intuition. The sound vibrations can help guide spirits to you and offers energy to the spirits. Once the singing bowl was being used, we could see shadows coming from the walls, all the way down the hall. We do not know who these spirits were, and we could only see them as shadow people.

The last room we investigated in was called the Trunk Room. In this room, the story is that a teacher was beaten. This again was a claim from a medium that visited the haunted location. So, we cannot claim this as an incident that actually happened in the building. We are not saying it didn't happen; we just like to have documentation to backup such instances. We know there are multiple horrific instances that go undocumented.

One of the groups that we were tagging along with had a piece of equipment that was able to monitor electromagnetic field, temperature, and vibrations (geophone). We had this set up on a shelving unit which was a very sturdy shelf, made with metal beams and wooden shelves. We were all either sitting or standing, far away from the shelving unit. We asked about the allegations in that room and started to get responses. The temperature was dropping, the geophone portion of the device was detecting vibrations, and the blue lights, which detect electromagnetic field, were blinking in response to our questions. We didn't solely focus on the allegations in that room, we just wanted to document that there was a possible spirit among us. We asked it to take the temperature from 57.0 to 56.0, and the spirit in the room granted our request. We asked them to light the blue lights bright, and they did.

We believe the activity we were getting was paranormal, and we can say that the old Rock Island YMCA is haunted. We just cannot say by whom and if the claims made about the abuse and the teacher being beaten are true.

JOSH AND KATIE HOPKINS

The Rock Island Arsenal – Quarters One

Previously used as a military quarter, the mansion was the second-largest residence in the federal government system. It was second to the White House.

Quarters One was formerly the home of the highest-ranking officer at the Rock Island Arsenal. It has 51 rooms and is 21,965 square feet.

Construction began in May 1870 under General Thomas S. Rodman and it was completed in 1872, under Major Flagler. The purpose of the quarters was to provide housing for the highest- ranking officer at the arsenal. It provided space for social gatherings, official gatherings and so on. Its architecture is a Victorian Italianate style. Quarters One is directly across from the

Confederate Prisoner of War Camp, which immediately gave the house a haunted feel.

The first major gathering was held in June 1871 for the funeral of General Rodman. The army decided to discontinue its services as a residence in 2006. The last occupants of the quarters were General and Mrs. Robert M. Radin, who left in 2008.

The Haunting of Quarters One

Quarters One is directly across from the Confederate Prisoner of War Camp, which immediately gave the house a haunted feel. Over 1,900 Confederate POW's died during the camp's existence. The camp was in existence for only twenty months.

Some of the claims are that people see a Confederate Prisoner of War leaning against the main posts at the entrance to the driveway of the residence. They say he is smoking a pipe, and is surrounded by the sound of drums.

There are many other spirits that are said to reside at Quarters One, and on the property. Of course, one of the most popular spirits is that of General Rodman. He died on June 7, 1871, before the residence was actually completed. He was the first commander to die on the Island, but his funeral would be the first public gathering in Quarters One. His funeral was in the parlors and he was considered the "Father of the Rock Island Arsenal."

There were many other commanders to pass away at Quarters One. In 1918, Colonel LeRoy Hillman, died as a result of the influenza epidemic. Another death in Quarters One was that of Colonel David King in 1932.

With the deaths of high-ranking officers and a POW Camp next door, there is a lot that triggers and aids the possibility of a haunting at Quarters One.

FINAL THOUGHTS

As we were writing this book, we tried to think of the many places that people may not know of or haven't visited. We wanted to address the urban legends of these locations and also shed some light on the real hauntings that are taking place there as well.

Our goal for this book was not to focus solely on the paranormal of each place, but also the rich history that they hold. It was in effort to highlight the incredible story that the Iowa Corridor (and the outskirts of the corridor) tells. This book only holds a handful of amazing places that are in Iowa. We hope you enjoyed the history, the urban legends and the true ghost stories of these incredible locations in the Iowa Haunted Corridor.

JOSH AND KATIE HOPKINS

ABOUT THE AUTHORS

Josh and Katie Hopkins were born and raised in the Iowa Corridor. They both have a passion for history and the paranormal. In fact, they met when Katie visited a historical location and Josh was the tour guide. They have both been involved, actively, in the paranormal since 2012, but they have had experiences with the paranormal for most of their lives. They have been to many haunted locations in the United States to investigate, the farthest they have traveled is to Old South Pittsburg Hospital in Chattanooga, Tennessee.

Josh's first ever investigation was at the Villisca Axe Murder House. His paranormal experiences have taken him on many journeys. He has also been featured on the YouTube shows *Beyond Existence* and *Paranormal Encounters*. He has also been featured on many local news stations and was on the Edinburgh Manor episode of *Ghost Adventures*.

Katie is an avid paranormal enthusiast and historian. She graduated with her Bachelor of Arts Degree in History (specialization in Civil War History) in 2010 from the University of Northern Iowa. She also has her Master of Science in Higher Education from Kaplan University. Katie has been featured on the YouTube shows *Beyond Existence* and *Paranormal Encounters*. She has also been featured on *My Ghost Story* when it was on the Bio Channel.

Josh and Katie have an amazing son and dog. They love to spend their time exploring when they can. Their paranormal adventures are far from over.

Other titles from Katie Hopkins:

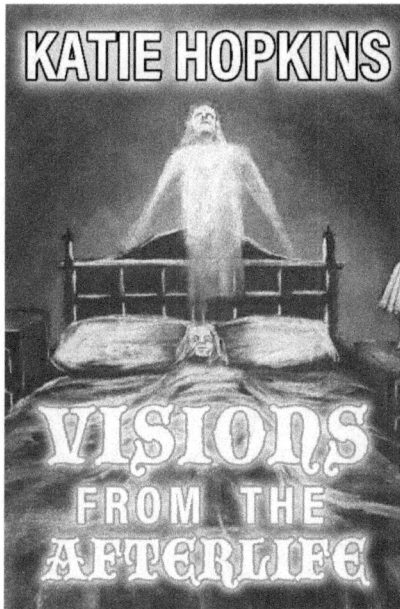

Visualizing spirits is the gift Katie Hopkins has been given as an Empath. Go on a journey with Katie to some of the most haunted locations in the Midwest and visualize the afterlife as Katie does.

* Dive deep into the meaning behind what dreams mean.
* Read personal experiences of signs from the afterlife.
* Learn about reincarnation and being born again.
* Learn characteristics that could be part of your past life.
* Learn about being greeted to the afterlife from a loved one.
* Decide if science can prove that the afterlife exists.

JOSH AND KATIE HOPKINS

For more information visit:
www.hauntedroadmedia.com

www.ingramcontent.com/pod-product-compliance
Lightning Source LLC
La Vergne TN
LVHW051415080426
835508LV00022B/3101